LIVING IN A
PLANT

DAVID CAFFREY

All correspondence to the author:
Email: livinginaplant@bigpond.com

© David Caffrey

First Printed 2020

The right of David Caffrey to be identified as the author of this work has been asserted by him in accordance with the Copyright, Designs and Patents act.

All rights reserved. No part of this publication may be reproduced, stored in or introduced into a retrieval system, or transmitted, in any form, or by any means (electronic, mechanical, photocopying, recording or otherwise) without the prior written permission of the publisher. Any person who does any unauthorised act in relation to this publication may be liable to criminal prosecution and civil claims for damages.

This book is sold subject to the condition that it shall not, by way of trade or otherwise, be lent, re-sold, hired out, or otherwise circulated without the publisher's prior consent in any form of binding or cover other than that in which it is published and without a similar condition including this condition being imposed on the subsequent purchaser.

WARNING:
This book contains language, material and events that may be considered prejudiced, stereotyped or offensive. They may not be the opinions, ideas, or beliefs of the reader. By choosing to proceed past this disclaimer, the reader accepts responsibility for how they react to the content contained herein.

ISBN: 978-0-6488348-0-9

CONTENTS

Acknowledgements ....*v*

Chapter 1	This Book and the Leg End 17
Chapter 2	Kick Off 21
Chapter 3	Herbert 27
Chapter 4	A Little Factory History 31
Chapter 5	First Contact 39
Chapter 6	Welcome the the Madhouse 45
Chapter 7	Culture Wars 59
Chapter 8	The Corner Shop 65
Chapter 9	The Night Shift 75
Chapter 10	Meet the Ladies 87
Chapter 11	Moving On (A Little About Home) 95
Chapter 12	The Cleaners 111
Chapter 13	Who's in charge? 121
Chapter 14	Shifting Apart 137
Chapter 15	Demolition Men 159
Chapter 16	A Bit About Mine 175
Chapter 17	Sick and Relief 189
Chapter 18	The End's in Sight 211
Chapter 19	To Sum Up 219
Chapter 20	...And Finally! 223

Bibliography *229*

Dedicated to the men and women who make stuff.

Acknowledgements

*"I don't see how you can write anything of value
if you don't offend someone."*
[Marvin Harris]

If you have decided to take the time to pick up and read this literary jumble sale, all about the last great British car producer, or the 'AUSTIN' as the locals called it, I would thank you in advance. If you have put your hand in your pocket and purchased it then thanks a million, and may you be blessed with a thousand camels. If you have 'acquired' a copy in some form or other, good luck to you. Just make sure, if it is in paper form, that you don't lick your fingers when you turn the pages. Not knowing the history of your particular copy opens up the possibility that previous owners may have been toilet readers. As a second hand book reader I am never far away from a bottle of alcohol hand wash…just saying.

When I sat down to write this small snatch of history I didn't think for one minute that I would finish it or be able to produce it in a readable form. Nevertheless I decided that I would give it 100% so my kids and maybe future relatives would have the chance to really see what life was like for me at a certain time in my history. I suppose then that my children have been the main driving force in its completion, and I hope it will paint a picture of what their old dad was like when he was a young fellah trying to make his way in the world.

It was never my intention to write anything popular or try to smash into the world of literature as the new JK Rowling. Fucking fat chance! This world appears, let's face it, as pretty much sewn up by a few well known certainties [No I don't mean celebrities]. Self publishing has of course changed the game a tad allowing anyone with a story to at least have a go.

I decided, as much as possible, to write as I spoke/speak and had ongoing disputes with spell check about this matter. I didn't realize how grammatically incorrect I was until that cheeky fucking light bulb insisted on tapping my screen every 30 seconds [Millenials please Google 'Microsoft cheeky fucking light bulb']. However we acted like adults and compromised on much of my assassination of the English language.

Those who know me have said that they can hear me telling them the story as they read, so I suppose I must have succeeded in some way to insert my personality within the words. Needless to say if you don't know me then this would not be the case for you. But to help you I would ask you to imagine a slight midland [English] dialect, wrapped around each word, not dissimilar to Ozzie Osborne or J.R Tolkien who was also a Brummie, of sorts.

You may on occasion get the impression from this read that I have some sort of infatuation with the toilet and that thing we all do, namely 'dropping anchor in pooh bay.' I would apologize to those who don't share my healthy [unhealthy?] interest in this important function, but to blokes of a similar mind, these are matters of both great conversational importance and humour material for the pub.

You may [or may not] be surprised to know that I do most of my reading and, in fact, penned much of this piece while sat on the throne, and do not apologize for it. But I suppose that I had better apologize for those long periods when the wife couldn't get in the lav. [Sorryluv!]

On reflection this could have caused a serious rift

in our relationship taking into account the quantity of visits she requires on a daily basis. I don't think it is just Tracy who has a bladder the same size as an acorn as life experience has shown me that the female urine retention system leaves a lot to be desired.

I once pointed this out as an audience member during a 'Jack Dee' [comedian] concert. I offered an observation on a pad he left during the break were I commented that during my life I reckon that I will spend a third of my time sleeping, a third of my time working and the remaining time waiting outside public lavatories while my wife has a piss. However, Jack Dee couldn't get his head around that one. Perhaps my comedic wit was far too advanced for he who has made a living out of the art of sarcasm?

This female inability to hold urine was backed up when I did the Looe [Ironic that this Cornish Town is my favourite holiday destination don't you think?] to Polperro walk with a female friend. About half way into the walk she got the urge to go 'wee wee' so we stopped off in Taland Bay. Now at the time Taland Bay was not the busiest place in the world, and apart from the café owner her dog and some sheep, there were not too many other life forms around.

I knew that there was a public lavatory on the main road, [I use the term 'main road' loosely as a centre line does not necessarily mean you can drive two cars both ways] and is effectively in the middle of nowhere. So, we headed in that direction. As we got to the toilet block I went straight into the gents, which was empty, but still stunk of piss. Would you believe it if I told you my female companion had to wait in the queue outside the ladies! You should, I was there, middle of nowhere, and a queue for the ladies!

Plastic surgeons need to pick up on this market

Living in a Plant

opportunity and offer an operation that would increase the size of the female bladder. What about the idea of a replacement of the female bladder with a basket ball, or something of a similar size and strength. Imagine the water we could save from the reduction in flushing. In poor rainfall countries they could offer it as a free service sponsored by 'Nike' or other well known sporting brands [You never know].

My dad, 'Paddy' on the other hand is on the other end of the scale. He has an Irish bladder that has the strength and resilience of Rhino skin. He has the ability to consume huge amounts of beer with very limited need for relief breaks. As a young man still living at home, I would wait outside the only family toilet for him to finish his business during a work day morning. I would listen in awe and amazement to the recent night's ale being emptied into the big white telephone.

He could stand there for 5 minutes creating a constant stream of waterfall type noise's, with the occasional break for breath and rasping fart. Just when you thought he had finished, he would start again. It was like a form of Chinese water torture, Irish water torture in fact!

On a visit to Canberra [Australia ,in case you didn't know] I met up with a Rural fire fighter who told me all about the problems they have with bush fires and getting water into the areas on fire. It was then that it hit me, they could strap my old man under a helicopter before his morning piss, and he could be used as an air mobile fire extinguisher. In fact if they utilized the Irish community appropriately, they would never have to worry about bush fires again. I mean, they could have a fleet of helicopters with highly trained Irishmen on standby in the local boozer to keep topped up in the event of a fire! My rural fire fighting buddy thought it was a great idea, once he had consumed a bottle of rum and his sober intellect had been put away for the evening.

Change the subject...

You can imagine, once you have read, how difficult it would be to interpret the different accents and dialects that I have included, which I think make all the difference to the tale. [Google can help with this] Local dialects in England are just an amazing freak of nature. You can walk over the next hill from any given location and find a local with a totally different way of saying the same thing as those you left behind. I have been all over the world to many places meeting many people and the one common factor that surprise's all those who have visited Blighty are the numerous dialects on offer.

Differing dialects are also prevalent in my new home Australia. My friends and associates from Queensland point this out when they explain that they are very different from those in New South Wales who 'talk like a bunch of cunts.'

One of the greatest sins committed by anyone, especially actors, are those who try to mimic accents or dialects without any form of training or guidance. This is especially white knuckle territory when a poor British or Irish accent is thrown about. That look you get when you try it without the utmost proficiency can never and should never be vocalized.

Film makers have absolutely no excuse. What is wrong with Liam, his holiness, Neeson playing the role of every Irish person on the big screen or just playing every role with his natural accent? Sean Connery did for his whole career ffs! Has he not already proved his flexibility to play every role in the known universe? Just to really take the piss, the makers of Star Wars get big Liam to put on a strange English accent as Qui-Gon Jinn! What a

24 ct diamond encrusted opportunity missed. How much better would the Pod racing scene have been with the big fellah shouting in his best Ballymena "Will ye look at dat little cunt droive noy!" How about Ewan Mac as Ben Kenobi, at the moment Liam gets skewered by light sabre before his very eyes, roars in his broadest jock cent at the Maul that is Darth "YOU YE SPIKEY HEEDED BASTARD! THAT'S MA FUKIN BUDDY! KEMERE!" and then proceeds to drop the Jedi nut.

Just missed opportunities, and frankly unfair, especially since Oliver Stone allowed Colin Farrell to play Alexander the Great using his native Dublin drawl. I was convinced. The idea of an angry drunk Irishman rampaging around Eastern Europe and Asia looking for a fight made perfect sense.

When I initially wrote everything down it was in handwritten form, which in itself must have been a challenge, bearing in mind my handwriting looks like it has been produced by a chimp holding the pen between the cheeks of its arse. But to try and work out what the fuck I was trying to say must have been a nightmare, but someone did it and I thank you Debs.

Debs and I haven't always been the best of friends, something to do with the throw away comment I once made in passing referring to her rear end and its size. But oh my, did I pay for it with silence for quite a while after. I could feel her hating me even when I wasn't with her or even in the same building. Women do hate really well, don't you girls! Anyway after a short while, well about 3 years of daggers and silence, we managed to put my, sorry, our differences behind us, and for that, I am very happy.

My mate Steve, who I worked with for 4 years in a previous life as a British Bobby, was also a big influence on my story telling, and he probably didn't even know. I would spend 10 hours a day with Steve, working, eating and sleeping together on many occasions. I would clarify that the sleeping was in the police car on nightshift when we should have been working, okay? Anyhow, I spent most of my waking time during that period with Steve, and probably saw more of him than I did of Tracy. Steve was and still is a great story teller having one for every occasion, and in the whole time that I worked with him he never ran out. This I found to be inspirational and may even push me to write something else. So, if you think this read is a load of crap then blame Steve.

When I first became associated with Steve all I knew about him was that he had transferred from a neighboring force and was ex-mounted unit. What I didn't realize was how significant that was until we popped to my house for a quick cup of tea during one of our first shifts together.

As we walked through the front door of my house, Steve noted a picture on the wall of Tracy's dad Rodney. It was taken while he was working as a steward at Aston Villa football Club and he managed to get in a photo with Andy Gray, the ex Aston Villa legend and TV pundit. When Steve asked about the picture I pointed out that it was Tracy's dad and told him about how he was killed working as a security guard at Coventry City FC [when they were a premiership club].

I will explain that Rod was sadly crushed by the Arsenal first team coach as it reversed into the car park at the old Coventry ground before kick off on match day.

Steve went a little quiet, but this was not because he was shocked by the association but the fact that he was on duty and sat on his horse within metres of Rod when the accident happened. It was the first time we had met face to face with someone who had such a clear explanation of the events around the incident.

Now, I am not a superstitious person, but up to that point, which was a few years after the incident, we never had a true explanation of what happened. The police investigation gave no explanation, and we got nothing from the coroner's court other than more questions. The health and safety people buggered up their case and our own legal types were about as much use as a safety switch on a suicide bomber's belt, until it came to the bill which was produced in a very efficient manner. What we didn't have and looked unlikely to get, and I will use the Americanism, was "closure", but Steve went a long way to providing it.

Now what are the odds of me and Steve coming together in the same working area, on the same team and working in the same role leading him to make that discovery at that time which was just at the end of the disappointing legal processes? I suppose that I could start reflecting about him being sent as a messenger etc etc, but I won't because I don't want Steve to rip the living piss out of me for the rest of his life.

It is fair to say that I should be thankful to the men and women at the factory who gave me a bucket full of material to write about. I have given you a snapshot of the place in the snippet in time that this read is set, but imagine how many stories there must be.

I used to hear people talk about how boring the job was and that this was the reason why they are paid so well, and to some extent I would agree with that view. But boring the place certainly was not. Sit at any yellow molded plastic table during break time or stand next to a group working or sipping coffee at a machine and you will hear a massive variety of views on a massive variety of subjects. You may not like them or agree but, if you are anything like me, you will listen.

Acknowledgements

It has been many years since I left the plant and I have seen a few of my old work mate's since but many more I haven't. It saddened me to see some of the older ones that used the factory family as their support, whether they knew it or not, fail to cope or even live very long once they retired or lost their jobs. On the other side of the coin many that left, thrived once the chains were cut and they realized that there was life and careers outside the factory walls.

John Towers and his mates at the Phoenix Consortium purchased the company for 10 quid in 2000 from BMW and perhaps there should be some thanks for trying to save a great British institution and extending its life just a little bit longer. I say British because even when the Japanese and the Germans came and tried to do whatever they wanted to do, it never changed the fact that the people building the cars were Brits of various types. It is a shame that they ultimately failed and rightly or wrongly criticism was directed at them from many angles. I like to think that Tower's was actually trying to save the company rather than make a quick buck. Perhaps I am a little naïve? I've got to say though, we Brits' probably have ourselves to blame.

I have owned 3 British made cars and I would put them at the top of my list of favourites. In contrast I have owned many more foreign cars and would not rate them above the British cars. Needless to say I am talking about mass produced cars, as I have never been in the elite car market. [Other than once owning a cherry pink Austin Mini 1000, cos who else in their right mind is gonna own that!] I have always tried to be positive about British design, manufacturing and engineering, and get thoroughly pissed off when I hear Brits' slagging our own products off.

Living in a Plant

The British are consistently guilty of making their own bad press and we continually pay the price as attitudes didn't change and businesses shut down. I suppose it must be part of the British, or is it English mentality to beat ourselves up. Don't! There is nothing wrong with being British, wherever you hail from. Many thousands arrive on British shores every year looking for the things we have taken for granted and more try to do it every year!

My cousin Brian had the right idea, as he went and lived in Germany, married a German, had 2 German kids and got himself a job as a German engineer. He can speak fluent German, but has retained his Britishness. On one particular occasion [or so the story goes] he was at work having a bit of a group meeting with his German colleagues, when one of them decided to pipe up and say in a particularly arrogant manner, " British engineers are not very good" or words to that effect. Not to be put down, Brian answers back in fluent German with a broad Brummie slant, "The fuckin' spitfire wasn't too bad was it mate!"

I think I had better finish off by apologizing for writing a piece that my relatives may want to read, but perhaps they shouldn't. This is predominately due to the language and some of the subjects that were discussed. But in my defence, I would suggest that we blokes have many discussions in bloke only environments that we would not want our family to know about. I have just decided to write mine down for you to read. Not to mention the fact that anyone who works in a factory would know it was a load of old bollocks without the fucking swearing!

It could be argued that this is a 'bloke' read for all the reasons stated. However, I would suggest that in an age of equality those who would suggest such could find themselves on the wrong end of a feminist slating. I am told that gender is a 'social construct' therefore I would like to add another 'B' to the ever growing list of genders. The definition of a 'Bloke' would be up for debate, so I will offer a few examples of my own to help you out;

- Any bloke who would admit to watching 'Countdown' would do so not because they wanted to have a go at the conundrum, but because they wanted to watch a really hot chick solving mathematical problems.

- If you took a poll asking blokes should a female tennis professional be awarded or deducted points for whipping her shirt off during a tennis match. I reckon you would not be surprised by the answer.

- You would never ask a bloke in front of his partner what would he/she [see what I did there!] do if they had to decide between never having a beer again and never seeing their partner again? Maybe not?

Nuff Said.

Longbridge Island - Heading to the Lickey Road.

CHAPTER 1

THIS BOOK AND THE LEG END

*"Dave will never amount to anything.
Thick Irish kids never do."*

[Anon 1985]

Those who are very smart and well read will quickly realise how this opus has evolved as the decades have past and my ability to string sentences together has improved [or not]. Like many great works that have taken decades to complete, so has this scribble. That would be the only comparison I would safely make between this story and a truly great literary work.

Two major hurdles conspired against me when I chose to start this working class historical record of factory life. One was clearly a self made hurdle and the other most certainly artistic snobbery and a class system.

Being as thick as fuck will ultimately offer a great deal of resistance when attempting to present a legible piece of artwork in book form. I was, and still am, to some degree a self confessed thick fuck. Writing 'fuck the pigs' on the back of the school boiler house in fat pen, takes a lot less thought than this mammoth task quite frankly. I am not saying that the British comprehensive school system failed me. More to the point, I would have probably been better equipped if I had bothered to turn up at lessons instead of smoking Benson and Hedges cigarettes in the alley ways adjoining the school.

Don't get me wrong, I was not a complete failure at school, and history and break time were always a must turn up for event. But nothing about the chalk and talk method of education ever inspired me. As it was I left school with nothing more than a need to get a job, any job and become part of Thatcher's capitalist success story. Sadly, what I didn't realise was that the old cow only allowed blue bloods into her club, so I had to find my own success the old fashioned way. Hard work, common sense and the sweat off my back were the tools I used to get on.

After little more than 12 months at the Rova' I began to realise that the world was full of aliens just like me. *But how the fuck do you rememeber every story, every person and every event?* Easy! Bob Monkhouse the British comedian was being interviewed on Parkinson or some other chat show event [I can't fucking remember!] and he explained how he kept a note book with him at all times and wrote everything down. That is exactly what I did! I did forget to write down what show it was that offered me this epiphany though. As a result, the years went by and I didn't miss a story.

Eventually I left the company in search of other shit, and while doing this other shit I met people who had a grasp of the English language, could read my notes and could type...and shit! It was at this point that I decided to venture into the world of best seller books and the numerous awards that would surely follow.

First up, I decided to contact a local Brummie [person from Birmingham] historian by the name of Carl Fuckin'Chinn. Reasons for his full name will become apparent. Carl was a local radio, TV and newspaper celeb who, I thought, would love to endorse such a personal and historically accurate snapshot of a local lad from the Rova'. So I flicked him a few emails, made contact and sent him a couple of chapters. I didn't expect to get any feedback but you have to be in it to win it.

At the same time I went through the phone book

Chapter 1 - This Book and The Leg End

[Millenials please see Google] and found a literary agent in Birmingham who gave me the number of an agent somewhere else who gave me a number for an agent in London who 'might be interested.' I called and spoke to a woman who sounded like someone out of a theatre production made for people who were really really posh. She advised me to send 3 chapters for her "perusal." After checking the dictionary and finding out what perusal meant, I sent it for her...perusal.

About two weeks later, me the wife and kids were sat in a Chinese restaurant, making short work of the all you can eat buffet. I was just about to go for another pint when I noticed my 6 year old lad was standing near the front door having a full on conversation with someone on my mobile phone brick.

Ahhhhh! I thought, *Look at him pretending to use the phone.* My calmness was suddenly overcome by fright as I realised that he may be on the phone to the emergency services or worse, he may have dialled one of the phone sex numbers on the cards pinned around the nearby public phone. Not that I was worried about the phone sex but the 50p per minute call costs would be hard to explain to the missus.

I calmly took the phone off him so as not to cause long term techno trauma, at which to my utter surprise he said, "Its Carl Chinn daddy."

"What have I told you about telling fucking lies?" I said not so calmly, but then noticed a voice on the end of the phone.

"Oroight Dave" came the greeting in broadest Carl Fuckin' Chinnian English.

Well, what a win. Not only did Carl love what he had read, he wanted to endorse the book on publication!

Not too long after this I decided to contact the agent

to see how her perusaling was going. Now I am not the sort of person to get offended by feedback, as long as it is fair and balanced. What I received was an assassination, not only about the grammar, but about the content. Apparently the content was 'not what the literary world is looking for.' I was quick to point out that the world didn't exist only in luvie wine bars and art exhibitions. My call was ended without any forward moving advice from the agent and it probably didn't help by calling her a stuck up old hag.

Not to be deterred, I decided to contact Carl Fuckin' Chinn. Surely he could point me in the right direction, since he was going to endorse the book. *Carl gets it*, I thought.

Well, email after email, call after call leaving messages proved me wrong. Eventually I spoke to CFC, [Takes too long to write Carl Fuckin'Chinn] and he decided that he couldn't endorse my scribble! So, deterred was what I became, and onto the back shelf went a masterpiece.

In the early 2000's I decided to spend some more time re-reading and updating the storyline, brought about by the news that the Austin plant was to be no more. I went for a self publishing company that looked very flash on the web, but turned out to be a money pit. Fortunately, I saw the pit before the money went in. What I did do was expand the story to fit current events and include a little more history.

More recently we now have the sad news that we are going to lose our vehicle manufacturing here in Australia. This has made me more determined to produce something that can enter the public sphere, so these stories and events are not forgotten. My hope is that maybe some of the men and women who worked in these manufacturing industries will produce their own stories.

CHAPTER 2

KICK OFF

"It takes a good dog to kill a badger!"
[Rod Reeves]

I hope you are not too confused as to what this book is actually about? Just to be clear, it's about a period of my life spent working in the Longbridge Car Plant in Birmingham, the one the Germans purchased so they could shut it down after telling everyone they wouldn't shut it down. From May 1990 to February 1995 I worked with some of the stupidest, smartest, ugliest, opinionated, unopinionated, most interesting and uninteresting people I have ever met.

Don't expect to get any technical information about cars or working practices, this is purely about people and the environment in which we worked. To be frank, above changing a tyre the internal workings of any motor vehicle is as understandable to me as the second and third episode of the "Matrix" or any Harry Potter movie ever made.

I have tried to describe the surroundings to the best of my abilities, and include as many people I could, stories I heard and conversations I have overheard or was told about. I make no apologies for artistic licence.

It was difficult, but I feel I have done the conversations justice and kept them as close to the real thing as my memory will allow. What I refused to do is alter the essence of the characters that I was exposed to on a daily basis, but capture in as much detail the types of personalities that were on display during my stint at the Rova plant.

It is perfectly reasonable to suggest that it could have

been set in any large manufacturing establishment and many of the characters could be found in any of those environments. But this is a personal view and recollection about my time at the Longbridge Plant which is important to me of course. As long as the content is interesting, makes you smile or even identify a stereo type in your own life, and you can fit the five to ten minute bursts of reading into your busy schedule, I have succeeded in what I set out to do.

As the story unfolds you will come to realize, if you haven't already, that this is by no means an intellectual read, the main reason being that I am not an intellectual and would never claim to be. In my defence, I did once manage to complete a crossword in a woman's magazine. The fact my wife had to help me spell a couple of the words that related to the monthly business does not deflect from the fact that I solved the clues by myself.

I enjoy observing people and talking about our strange human quirks, natural behaviour, and the activities that we try to conceal from each other or pretend not to indulge in. Things like looking at your arsehole in the bedroom mirror so you know what it looks like, or is that just me? Every single human is funny in some way, and if you haven't considered this view then spend some time somewhere in public and watch strangers. If you don't fancy this just study the people you know and work with. Try getting yourself some wraparound sunglasses to wear in order to avoid possible assault by strangers or intervention by the local authorities.

In a nut shell, that's all this book is about: people and my observations of a group during a certain period of time, splattered with some home life and a little history.

One of the funniest people I knew didn't even realize he was funny and made me laugh just by looking at him

Chapter 2 - Kick Off

and his human habits. A thirty-something at the time, Mark had recently split from his defacto and was living in his local authority owned bachelor pad. We worked together for a couple of years, but stayed friends once our work circumstances changed. He was a teenager during the early seventies and his dress sense and style remained in that era. Even his speech was seventies-esque! He lived in a basement flat with his three cats and I would visit on a regular basis, sometimes sneaking in through the back door just to see him jump. I did it so often that he became a nervous wreck! "I even check the back of the fuckin' shitter now, just in case you jump out when I'm havin' a dump!" he would moan.

One day I decided to give his heart another jolt, so I climbed in through his kitchen window. Lowering myself onto the sink and washing surface, I noted that Mark was nowhere to be seen. I moved stealthily into the living room, trying to be as quiet as a mouse so that I could maximise the shock effect. As I passed the bathroom I heard moaning and gentle splashing of water. The moaning seemed to change pitch, giving the impression of different people making the noises, and they sounded like people having something very nice done to them!

Fukin'el, I thought, *He's got 'imself a bird in the bathroom!* I stood in the kitchen doorway opposite and listened as the noises became more frantic and the splashing got louder. I even made myself a cup of tea. *I'll have to have a look at this bird* I thought.

Now please don't think that I am some sort of weird voyeur, when I am in fact a very normal voyeur. Just try to understand that it had been a very long period between Mark leaving his defacto and finding a new companion. Not to mention the fact that he wasn't the world's best looking dude. As a result, I was more interested in seeing what this stranger actually looked like. I didn't want him bullshitting me that he just banged Birmingham's answer to Bo Derek, [Millennials refer to Google] when she actually looked like a really shit professional boxer.

Ultimately the moaning stopped and a pair of feet hit the bathroom floor, closely followed by the sound of a door opening. He was walking in my direction. "FUCKIN' TWAT!" He screamed as he jumped back five feet without bending his knees. The door behind him swung open and I saw that the bathroom was empty. The penny dropped: *Aahh*, I thought, *Madam Palm and her five lovely daughters have been for a visit.* "How long have you been there you fuckin' bastard?" He screamed. "Oh, only about ten minutes" I replied with a grin.

Needless to say, I was not allowed back for a while and was very lucky to get out with my teeth intact.

Even though you may not see much evidence of it so far, I tried to stick to a plot, but thought *Fuck it* at about page 17. However, I am fairly certain that you will be able to follow my ramblings easily enough. Frankly, if you have got this far, you will be OK. I hope some of the contents make you smile for a while at least, and maybe you will identify someone in the book as a person in your own life.

I do not apologize for any stereotypes, because people can be stereotypical. Men do 'men' things, women do 'women' things (such as buying facial wash gel with gritty bits and leaving it in the shower so that blokes pick it up thinking its shower gel and subsequently remove half their skin before realizing!). That being said these are my opinions, and seeing it with your own two eyes and knowing it for a fact isn't always evidence enough for some progressive types. If you are struggling up to this point, go and get a refund, or put the book back behind the toilet roll holder.

Chapter 2 - Kick Off

My story covers a period in history when rave/house music was the noise on the radio and in the clubs, Freddie Mercury died and Milli Vanilli lip synced their way to the top of the pop world, and all the way back to the bottom. Operation 'Desert Storm' raged, and the Conservatives continued to rule. Paul 'Gazza' Gascoigne cried his heart out at every opportunity at the Italia 90 world cup. President George Bush Senior started the new world order, followed by Bill Clinton who proceeded to take the "no smoking" signs down in the White House. The internet goes live and humans subsequently begin to lose the ability to talk to each other. We spoke to each other in person most of the time and even stupid people could spell, knew what a pen was and could write by hand. Not one person I knew had a mobile phone [Imagine!!!]. We listened to music on a walkman and fucked up numerous music audio tapes when the tape would get stuck in the turny thing inside. Nelson Mandela gets parole and is rehabilitated well enough to become the president of South Africa and finally...after centuries of Britain keeping the French at bay behind the English Channel, the tunnel is finished.

I'm sure many other things happened that I probably missed when buried in the noise and the dust of the factory. I was in my early twenties at the time I joined the fray, still learning about life and couldn't have chosen a better place to continue my education.

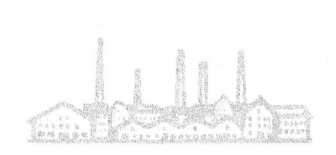

CHAPTER 3

HERBERT

"Even among the cognoscenti, few are likely to mention a farmer's son called Herbert Austin; yet he was one of the most ingenious and technically influential of them all."

[Gavin Bennett]

Herbert was born on the 8th of November 1866 in Buckinghamshire, England. At the age of 4 he moved with his family to South Yorkshire where his old man got a job working for a really posh bloke as a Bailiff.

At a very young age it was noted that Herbert was very good at drawing, not dissimilar to me in fact. However, I chose to draw comic characters whereas Herbert was drawing mechanical objects of a quality way beyond his tender years. If only I had picked up the Auto Trader instead of the Beano, I could have been a millionaire.

As a result of his aptitude with the pencil, it was decided that he should be an architect, so his mother's brother's posh bloke's friend, set him up with an apprenticeship as such. This didn't go too well as Herbert loved his machines, and he subsequently was told off and had the apprenticeship canned. While he and his parents were trying to set up something more suitable, Herbert's uncle arrived from Australia, and as luck would have it, he was a big knob at an engineering firm down under. With ma Austin on his side, Herbert was able to convince pa Austin that a hiking trip around Australia would be a great learning experience.

After two months on a boat Herbert arrived in Melbourne. [I moan about 27 hours on a plane, Jaysus!].

In true Aussie fashion, by his second day he was down the races watching the 1884 Melbourne Cup, and no doubt would have been amazed at how the beautifully attired men and women who arrived at 10am, turned into skanky moles by 3pm after consuming too much alcohol. Mores the pity that he isn't alive today as I am sure Herbert would have come up with better solutions for relieving yourself than standing in a blue plastic box full of dirty toilet paper, and waiting for an hour to buy overpriced crap beer presented in a plastic cup!

Unlike yours truly, who carried on with the task of punching on with drunken Australians instead of drunken brits, Herbert set about fulfilling his destiny as a great designer and improver of all things mechanical. Fredrick Wolseley, a famous industrialist in his own right, saw the potential in Herbert and opened the doors that facilitated Herbert's design improvements in the sheep shearing industry. Such was his success; Herbert was offered a directorship of Fred's UK company. So in 1893, with his new Aussie wife in tow, Herbert returned to Blighty.

On his arrival back in Birmingham, Herbert set about transforming the company into a manufacturer of Motor Vehicles. His first was a three wheeler and could be purchased for 110 quid for a two seater or 150 quid for a four seater. It also came with a 6 month guarantee!

In 1898 he drove one of his vehicles to Rhyl in Wales, a distance of 225 miles at an average speed of 8 miles per hour. How ironic that more than 100 years later, this is about the average speed most families attain when they decide to drive to the coast from the cities.

Herbert wanted to expand the ability of the company to build motor vehicles, but needed more cash. In stepped Vickers Sons and Maxim to invest, and Herbert was duly appointed General Manager. You would imagine that this

Chapter 3 - Herbert

amount of success and opportunity would be enough for any person. However, Herbert wanted to build his own cars, "In a sense it is possible that I made a mistake when I took over management of Wolseley Company for Messrs Vickers, in that I did not commence to build cars on my own account. It would, of course, have had to be in a very small way, but it might have been better from the personal stand point than managing somebody else's business. It would have been a slow process, however, and also somewhat unsafe."

Disagreements about engines, and no doubt other matters resulted in Herbert leaving his job, but not after he received high praise and thanks from his ex-employers. Notwithstanding that as a result of Herbert's efforts and vision, the same company went on to be one of the biggest motor vehicle producers in the world.

Herbert went it alone, and by 1906 produced his first motor vehicle in sleepy Longbridge. I'm sure with an amount of pride Herbert pulled out of the factory in the number 1 vehicle and took off up Lickey Road, soon to be followed by hundreds of thousands of others.

I was going to suggest that he probably knocked out a few doughnuts since traffic would have been pretty scarce. This would of course be utterly inaccurate as it was Herbert who suggested at a time when road rules where just emerging, that the rule of thumb for drivers should be 'Courtesy and common sense.' Perhaps advice that all drivers should have imprinted on whatever licence to drive they carry.

There would be so much more to say about this great industrialist, but this is not a biography, and I do not have the literary prowess to do his life justice.

CHAPTER 4

A LITTLE FACTORY HISTORY

"History never changes, it just keeps repeating itself."
[A very clever person]

Between 1895 and 1901 a company by the name of 'White and Pike Ltd' who were involved in the copper plate print business, set up the beginnings of the factory in Longbridge at a cost of 105,000 quid. This business failed and the bank repossessed. [How prophetic]. In 1905, in stepped Herbert.

Herbert purchased the derelict site that was the copper plate printing company, in addition to quite a few more acres of what was then rural land, for the discount price of 7,500 quid. By 1912 the factory covered 8 acres, had 1800 employees, with a night shift and was banging out 1000 cars per year. In 1914 the company was floated on the stock market and raised 250,000 quid in shares. Nice work Herbert!

Through the Great War production turned to help the war effort. The workforce grew massively as a result, and such was the need to move people from the city of Birmingham to fill the jobs, Longbridge train station was born. They even built an airfield at Cofton Hackett, just up the road, for the testing and launching of the 2000 aeroplanes that were subsequently built. Incredible numbers me thinks. This on top of the 8000 shells, 650 guns, 2000 trucks and 2500 aeroplane engines!

Opposite what was the North Works is the Austin Village, created by Herbert and built in 1916. The Great War raged and the number of employees swelled to five figures in order to meet the new demands of wartime production. Due to house-building being suspended, Herbert decided to import prefabricated bungalow kits from the USA, and in 1917, the red cedar bungalows arrived and were erected with 25 pairs of brick-built houses interspersed to act as a fire break.

Some historians believe that many more were ordered, but were lost as the Atlantic fleets were attacked and sunk. One particular story goes that, against advice, all the lids had been loaded onto one ship and the sides onto another. The ship with the lids was sunk, and this caused an obvious construction problem! Anyway, the new structures provided warmth and dry beds for the workers and were fitted with modern fitments for the time.

The war ended and the work force predictably shrank as the company re-modernized to provide peacetime goods, so the need for the extra housing disappeared. The bungalows were sold to private buyers for £250 leasehold or £300 freehold and rented by families. They were only meant to be temporary buildings, but have been so well maintained that they are still there today, demanding a high price due to the beauty of the area and their unusual nature. The site has gradually been surrounded by the city, and modern shithole-type estates, but it has not been spoiled (thankfully) and is now known as the Austin Village Trust.

My wife had family living in the Trust, and her great uncle Lol [God rest his soul] gave many years service, from the age of fourteen, only broken by his service during World War II. I was told by older employees during my time at the factory, of a time when your whole life revolved around the company, it being your employer, insurer, entertainer, landlord, and eventually your old age provider in the form of the company pension.

Chapter 4 - A Little Factory History

Every year in early May the locals living in the Trust organize a Fete, which, in all the years I have been forced against my will to go, has never been rained upon. In fact I can't recall a time when I wasn't sweating buckets! The whole of the street is blocked off at both ends and the occupants of the houses set up stalls outside their garden gates selling odds and ends, plants, home-made cakes, bric-a-brac etc. Some will set up fairground games where you throw balls at a target to win prizes. The same faces would appear every year, usually with last year's homemade game that people pay to play. The best (worst) had to be 'Splat the Rat'. This game consisted of a two-foot plank of wood with a box at one end. A piece of string has a rag attached at one end, the other being fed through the box and held by the controller of the 'rat'. The player holds a wooden hammer and attempts to hit the rag, sorry 'Rat' before the controller can pull it into the box. I can only put it down to utter boredom that drove the punters to pay to play, because this was the most exciting thing to do. I can't say I ever saw anyone win.

It's probably fair to say that it is was a very environmentally friendly affair due to the fact that most of the stuff purchased ends up on a different table next year for someone else to buy. Additions to the fete have been the Majorettes and the now compulsory 'Bouncy Castle'. Another compulsory event with the arrival of my two kids is that at least one of them ended up with dog shit on their shoe! But, in all fairness, it retained its innocence and had not been invaded by the 'professional car-booters', still safe in the hands of the residents of the Trust.

By 1919 the factory was 10 times its pre-war size, and Herbert and his workers continued to build vehicles, tractors, trucks and aeroplanes. When the Second World

War arrived, Herbert and his workers, including hundreds of women as with the Great War, were once again called into action.

Armour piercing rounds were produced, along with depth charges and mines. Bren guns and mortars were produced in the west works where I ended up decades later. This is something that frankly scares me shitless when you think of some of the characters I met in my time and you will meet as you move on. Who, if born a few years earlier...no, let it go!

Hurricane fighters and bomber aircraft, numbering up to 3000 were built! And if that wasn't enough they also produced helmets and jerry cans.

I can still remember the older fellahs who had been at the factory since the 60's talking about the 'Beau fighter line' at Trentham. Such a shame it took nearly 30 years and Wikipedia to enlighten me as to what they were talking about.

In 1946 the factory had managed to build its one millionth car! In 1952 the 'Morris' entered the fray and so Austin Morris was born. Then, in 1968 the socialists decided to remove Herbert from the company banner, and so was born 'British fucking Leyland.' It all went downhill from this point. By 1975 the money men got worried and the Government had to step in and become a major shareholder. 'Red Robbo' came, saw, and got 'everybody out!' Eventually he was got out, and only 600 of the 14000 workers voted to strike in his favour. He was a communist after all, not to mention a 'yam yam.' [All will become clear].

As the world developed and other countries continued to develop the ability to produce cars cheaper, the 'Austin' as it was still fondly called, had to change and compete. Needless to say, the workforce shrunk as the years went

Chapter 4 - A Little Factory History

on. Robots and machines replacing men accelerated the reduction to a level of about eleven thousand at the time I joined. But even then, as now, local communities existed and all manner of businesses relied on the money produced directly or indirectly by the plant.

To help in the transition from the mass producer of bin skips with wheels to a return as a world-beating car manufacturer, Maggie T. sold the company for about a shilling to British Aerospace, turning it into a PLC. Thus it was that the financial burden of a 1970's strike-ridden company was removed from the hands of the taxpayer. This was clearly done in the hope that BA would turn it into a profit-maker.

The 'Rover Group' as it was renamed, was going through yet another transitional period at the start of my employment with them, and it was due to the changes that the work force was being increased, and my opportunity to gain employment came about. The same as any large company, the Rova' went through numerous changes in its history, as you can imagine. This time it was all about progress, and to be able to cope and compete within the private sector. Since the days of 'Red Robbo' and 'British Leyland', the company had been trying to have a major image change which was essential if they were to survive as a major car producer in a competitive Global market.

At the time I still recall the roads being full of rusty models such as the Montego, Maestro and Metro, and worst of all, the scrap yards still contained large quantities of Austin Allegros, Maxis, and the Princess. What an unbelievable array of crap cars! I mean, how many people would think that a square steering wheel was a good idea? I am not joking...Google it!

Not long before I started, the New West building had been built and opened by the Prince of Wales. This new

Living in a Plant

structure was similar to other modern factory buildings and was now mixed in amongst the dusty old caverns built when Queen Victoria was still on the throne. All the buildings were stitched together so the flow of production was continuous. Substantial antique spiked railings ran the perimeter of the plant sweeping up to the new modern signs displaying the company emblem.

Situated on the border of the City of Birmingham and county of Worcestershire next to Lickey Hills Country Park, you could leave a smokey, dirt-filled environment and walk no more than ten minutes into some of the most beautiful countryside you could hope to find. To their credit, the company did a great deal to keep the area clean, and responded positively to local complaints. One in particular I remember being the smell of paint during the day. How they rectified it, I don't know, but they did.

Not only did the company look to change the image of the plant and products, but it also looked to change the image and attitude of the workforce. Each employee, management included, was issued with made-to-measure jacket and trousers with the company name emblazoned across the chest. This was a far cry from the bib and braces days of years gone by.

No! Now you looked like a member of a professional organization, just like the Japanese in their Far Eastern factories and the new plants being erected by the Japanese all over the North of England. We too had our very own contingent of Japanese who came from our new partners, Honda. Now they would be entwined in the long history of the Longbridge! Would they survive?

Total Quality Improvement (TQI) was the buzzword; a means to change the way the established workforce went and thought about their work. The management strived to gain the 'Investors in People' Award, eventually succeeding.

Chapter 4 - A Little Factory History

There were hundreds of new workers indoctrinated into the new philosophy, young, vibrant and eager to work (yeah, right!). Everything was put in place to turn the company into a world-beater. But who would win the battle? Would the management succeed, or would the old attitudes come through and absorb the new workers?

CHAPTER 5

FIRST CONTACT

*"It's a pretty safe working environment,
just watch out for that cunt Tipper!"*

[A gaffer]

"You used to be ever so thin and healthy when you worked at the fruit and veg shop." My girlfriend Tracy looked at my flabby structure with a smile that said she was not overly impressed with the way I had let myself go, but she was right. After twelve wasted months of trying to be a self-employed entrepreneur (which had failed miserably), I went on to spend four months milling about, watching videos, smoking heavily, eating the wrong food and drinking copious quantities of the wrong liquids. I had become everything I had always despised. Unfit, unhealthy and lacking any motivation. The weight was wrapping itself around me like a warm blanket. I looked like a beached whale as I lay on the bed in my underpants, unable even to put my socks on without huffing and puffing.

Looking back, I have nothing but sympathy for poor Tracy, due to the fact that when we were in the throes of passion I would suffocate her with my substantial cheeks, those on my face that is. It was a problem that was to take years to overcome, mainly due to my refusal to see what I had become. Instead of the eleven stone greyhound with the ability to carry 100lbs of spuds on my back up and down flights of stairs, I had deteriorated into a mess.

It was mid-February 1990 and I had reached a crossroads in my life; out of work and not looking to go back to a seventy-hour week in the fresh produce industry labouring for shit money.

Worst of all, I had become a ponce, living off Tracy's earnings as a nurse. Due to Maggie Thatcher's boom and bust policies it was unlikely that the recession we were in was going to allow me to get a job easily. With mounting debts we were in danger of losing our one bedroom unit in the sleepy Rednal district of Birmingham and I could see no way out of the fix we were in.

I was saved by a friend who told me the Rover Group at the Longbridge site were looking to hire new blood to build the new range of cars they were planning. So as quick as my fat arse would carry me, I went down to the personnel offices situated by Longbridge traffic island and filled out an application form. Bugger me if they didn't call me down for an interview within two weeks, giving me my first taste of the things to come.

I would venture to say that if I asked you what your idea of a job interview was it would be nothing like what I experienced on the morning of mine. I walked through the shabby double doors into a cigarette smoke-filled waiting area with sixty or more other prospective employees sitting around on the plastic chairs provided.

"Come for an interview 'ave ye' luva?" enquired the smiling middle-aged woman behind the counter marked 'RECEPTION'.

"Yeah, err, 10:30," I replied, still a little taken aback by the quantity of my opponents for the job. I handed her my appointment card which she duly dropped ash onto from the burning cigarette lodged in her mouth. Without looking at it she threw it onto the pile of other cards scattered about on her desk.

"Tec' a seat dahlin', I'll give ye' a shout in a minute." She pointed to one of the chairs lined against the

Chapter 5 - First Contact

waiting room wall, and I did as I was instructed.

Prior to my arrival I had shit, showered, shaved and shampooed, put on a smart-but-casual shirt, thinking, *I'll make an effort seeing as though it's an interview*. I mean, you want to give yourself the best chance don't you? Okay, my blazer was a bit short on the sleeves and my trousers were a bit snug due to the extra bits of me I had added over recent times, but I was looking smart. As I looked at the others around me it became clear that I was the only one with this idea. Many, well pretty much *all* of the people around me looked as if they had just got out of bed and turned up.

The place looked more like an inner city benefits office than an interview waiting room. Some of my 'opponents' looked at me from where they sat and I read the stares as 'Who the fuck does he think he is?' making me more than a little self-conscious!

"Alroight kidda" the voice came from the bloke next to me, "Lookin' smart, just gorrup me, day even 'ave a chance te wash."

I was just about to say "No shit?" in my most sarcastic voice when:

"Come fe a gaffer's job 'ave ye?" he asked, and I duly enlightened him that I was there in the same capacity as him.

"Watcha' all fuckin' dressed up for then ye silly cunt?" he looked at me as if I had just told him that an alien had just shit on the steps of 10 Downing Street. However, the woman at the reception desk saved me from the monotony of explaining myself.

"Ye' can goo in now, Luva." She indicated to a door directly opposite her counter. I got up and went for the door, eager to escape the dirty fuckin' breath monster next to me.

As I walked into the room I was greeted by my interview panel: one with a grunt, the other with a smile. Both appeared to be hard-faced middle managers in their fifties who enjoyed the little power they had. Both had a thick head of hair in a seventies 'Elvis' style, though one was jet black, the other ginger - quite a contrast.

Straightaway I picked up it was going to be good guy - black hair, bad guy - ginger hair interview.

"Sit yer'self down son."

I did.

"So, why do ya want to join the Rova' Group?" asked black hair, at which I unloaded my rehearsed answer to an obvious question. It was full of bullshit about seeking a career with a forward-looking company etc etc, and when I had finished with the best beaming smile I could produce...

"That's a loada' BULLSHIT!" said Ginger in a 'don't take me for a twat' kind of voice, "you know as well as we do that you need a job te get ya off the dole, and we are the only ones employin'! Correct?"

To say I was a little taken aback would be an understatement, but I kept my composure and referred him to the question I had just given. The hours listening to 'Prime Minister's Question Time' had not been wasted.

Silence fell for a short spell as both looked down and made a note of something on the identical Rover Group clipboards they held. Black hair looked up once from his board, with a false smile of encouragement.

"Roight, David," continued Black Hair, "If oi was te show ya 'ow te put four screws into a square plate with four 'oles in it, 'ow lung would it take ya te do it on yer own?"

Are you taking the piss? I thought.

"Well, show me once and that would be enough." I

Chapter 5 - First Contact

replied with a look of obviousness on my face.

"I should fuckin' 'ope so!" exclaimed Ginger, and I imagined punching him full in the face. Silence fell again as the scribbling continued.

"So, woi should we pick you, David?" asked Black Hair, once again breaking the silence.

Have you seen the fuckin' monkeys outside? I thought, but proceeded with my rehearsed answer to another obvious question. As I finished, Ginger mumbled an inaudible comment into his pad and Black Hair said:

"Thanks David, goo and see Jackie at Reception and she'll tell ya what to do next."

So that was it. Five minutes long, three and a half of which I had filled with waffle.

I walked outside and was directed to the nurse's station to undergo a company medical that consisted of urinating into a pot (which is always too small) and reading a few letters off a card on the wall. The hearing test was ticked if you acknowledged the nurse when she called you in.

Finished, I walked out of the double doors I had gone in through, only to meet 'Breath' on the way out:

"I'll keep me eye out for ya at the induction, mebe we can sit togeva ay?"

Fuck off smelly! I thought. "Yeah, okay mate," I replied.

I headed back to my flat which was a fifteen minute walk away. I looked back and wondered to myself, what I was letting myself in for, yet realizing that I had no other options at that time.

The plant covered an area the size of a small town and was steeped in history, both good and bad. I had heard the rumours, but was about to find out if they were true, because within a few days I had received my letter confirming the offer of employment.

Personnel Office - Where I met Mr Smelly!

CHAPTER 6

WELCOME TO THE MADHOUSE

"Once you're in, you're in for life son."

[H]

It was the day after the May Day Bank Holiday that I started, so my first week lasted only four days, two days of which were spent in the Austin Social Club filling out numerous forms full of what appeared to be useless information. Then and to this day I still wonder what they needed most of it for or where in the name of Jehovah's arsehole it all ended up. Nothing was computerised, everything was on paper. I even met an old school friend who I had not seen for many years, who coincidentally was in a similar situation to me at the time. Fortunately, I did not come across the breath monster.

Once these monotonous tasks had been completed I moved to the 'Training Room' which was situated in the 'Old West' plant. I use the description 'Training Room' as it was so called, when it was in fact a holding area for new employees while you waited for somewhere to go. Every now and then a 'Gaffer' would appear from somewhere and enquire if anyone had any skills related to his given area. If no one was suitably qualified he would take volunteers who would be swept away into waiting vehicles.

As I sat and watched, it all reminded me of one of those scenes from a dusty American Border Town where a large group of natives would be hanging around chatting. The silence would be broken by a pick-up truck arriving, and a sun-glassed dude would pick out who he was going

Living in a Plant

to take for a day's work. Obviously, the difference being no work, no pay, for the natives, but with me, I'd just sit on my plastic chair, have another smoke and free Max Pax Coffee, and wait for the next truck to come along, all at the company's expense...Marvelous!

However, I had to volunteer for something, and since it was likely that the Managing Director's job would be unavailable for a while, I decided to go for 'logistics' - or 'stores' to you and me. It was at this point that I met probably the most memorable character I was to come into contact within the four-and-a-half years I was employed there.

His name was (and hopefully still is) Jim Thompson. He had many nicknames: Jim, Jimbo, Tomo, Sweaty Sock and many more that could only be used in the appropriate company. Jim was from North of the border and had a smooth rather than hard-edged Scottish accent. He was about 5ft10 with a full head of jet black hair which was a surprise, bearing in mind he was in his late fifties! He was questioned on numerous occasions about the source of the colour, but he swore it was au natural. This was put to the test on one occasion when he left the dye on a bit too long and his hair went sort of a very dark blue colour. Jim being Jim he stuck to his guns and made up some bullshit reason which I can't remember. He wore a thick pair of National Health Service glasses with the obligatory piece of tape holding the frame to the lens.

Jim was an old-fashioned gaffer who was in charge and made sure everyone knew it. But he was also friendly and approachable. He opted to wear a dirty white doctor's coat instead of the new company overalls.

He had many unhappy supervisors who all tried and failed to get him to conform to the new image. In the end it took about 2 years before he changed and this had more

Chapter 6 - Welcome to The Madhouse

to do with running out of his old overalls than wanting to conform.

When he administered a bollocking it was in a way that unnerved you, even scared those with a weak character! With an insane tantrum, filled with expletives in his native tongue, and plenty of finger-pointing, he would stamp his authority on new starters early in their careers. After a while, his tack would change to a soft, friendly approach, guiding you through what he wanted from you. But always and at any moment he could launch his tirade of abuse if things were going pear shaped.

"Yall reet son? Ma name is Jim Thompson", he held out a friendly hand and I received a genuine squeeze, "Come on and al tek ye up the deck an find 'e somey te dee". I rose from my seat and followed. We walked out of the training room along the length of the 'Old West' building. It was a Thursday, mid-morning and the place was buzzing with delivery trucks of all sizes, forklift trucks, cars and pedestrians coming and going. Electric flat-bed trucks (peddy trucks) whizzed past loaded with plastic crates full of bits of metal destined for who knows where.

I will explain that the Old and New West buildings were concerned with the putting together of all the bare metal bits of the car. Metal would arrive in bits and like giant jigsaws they would be glued, welded, bolted and fitted together then shipped off to the other parts of the factory to be turned into cars. "What ye dee afore ye came tee this madhouse?" Jim's question broke the silence and my day-dreaming as we walked.

"Err, I was a retailer," I simplified my answer to avoid a long drawn out explanation of my history.

"Oh eye, I did a bit o that me sel' when I was younger."

It will become apparent as my tale progresses that

Living in a Plant

Jim did just about *every* kind of job known to humankind, all of which had a story attached. In fact, I would suggest that during my time working with him, he covered the four corners of the globe as an employee in some guise or other, in his previous life. I would not for one minute suggest that he was being less-than-honest, but will let you decide for yourselves as the story continues.

We walked along the roadway between the Old and New West buildings eventually coming to the far corner of the New Building overlooking the Bristol Road South. Here we came to a 10 metre high roller shutter door made of canvas cut into the wall of the building. To the right of the canvas door was a pedestrian entrance door protected by a metal rail and it was this door that we used to gain entry to the building. From outside the noise was like any normal busy road with the hum of car noises and people, but as we stepped inside I was overwhelmed by a wall of noise that hit my ears, almost deafening me. The stench of heat, smoke and carbon attacked my nostrils straight away and I coughed for a little while until my senses adapted to the new surroundings.

From the outside, the New West building was impressive in size, but as you step into it, the enormity of the place becomes apparent. Mixed with the noise and the smell, it took me a few moments to take it all in. I had never seen anything like it before: hundreds of people busily going about their business, scores of welders working at speed joining bits of metal together causing bright mountains of sparks to fly through the air like cheap fireworks exploding. The place was busy with more fork-lifts and peddy trucks whizzing back and forth as men with walkie-talkies ran up and down the line followed by people scribbling on company clipboards.

I looked up into the cavernous surroundings which

Chapter 6 - Welcome to The Madhouse

seemed to be full of movement of materials and activity, and I likened it to an ant hill with everyone working together to produce a single end product. I could taste the fumes and dust in my mouth, the flavour that took a long time to get used to, and the smell which I can still remember today. It wasn't until you walked out and washed yourself down that the aroma left you for a short while until you returned.

As much as the cleaners tried to keep the place clean, everything you touched had a layer of dust on it that would attach itself to your clothes or hands from the slightest contact. Those that could spell, and even those that couldn't, would write some insulting comments on the dirty surfaces. Putting anything down on any surface guaranteed a coating of blackness especially clothes if you were stupid enough not to use the company overalls.

Keeping to the left of the building, we walked up the aisle that separated the workstations from the stores. The stores were now running to my left and parallel with the outside wall of the building. Huge crash barriers, probably 50 feet high, skirted the stores to prevent pallets stacked 40-50 feet high from falling onto the workers below. We followed the line of the stores, coming to a computer station with sit and reach trucks working in a protected area. This was the 'fifth aisle', and was used for storing smaller pallets of material. Next to it was the Automated Panel Store (APS), a huge labyrinth of pigeonholes containing material deposited and removed by automated lifts controlled by workers in a small office a little further along.

Finally we arrived at the 'Deck', or goods receiving area, as it was officially known. Again, on my left, pallets and materials were stacked high against the walls. In the middle of this was a toilet block with lockers for the workers, and on a level above was the drivers' restroom which overlooked the factory floor. To my right was a railway line! Oh yes, a fucking railway line! Dug into the floor, it allowed a train with five coaches to enter the building to be loaded and back-filled. As we walked the noise of the train filled the air and I stood back in amazement at the size of it all.

We reached the top of the building where the supervisors' offices were situated and the Road Receiving area was situated. Three large roller-shutter doors were in use with articulated trucks arriving in and out with more material. This place was huge, noisy, and very smelly!

"Hang on here a wee minute son," Jim left me standing at the end of the first bay with the train behind me. I saw two offices on the Road Deck, one quite large about 15 x 20 feet made out of metal panels, and to the extreme left of the roller doors in between the bays was a smaller office (about 8 x 10 feet) made of similar construction. These were the 'Road Receiving Offices', and Jim headed for the larger of the two.

I stood and wondered how long I would be here. I didn't like it much. I had become number 119049 on the company list and that made me feel like one of the ants. I did not want to be an ant! *This is just a stop gap*, I thought to myself, *until I sort myself out, get back on my feet*. I had debts to pay so I comforted myself with the thought of stability for a while, but I was not going to end up here until retirement and die 12 months afterwards like those I had heard about.

My head was so filled with other things, that I did not see the danger approaching. "Look out!"

The words made me jolt into action, just in time to see a pallet of car side-panels heading towards me at speed. I jumped back out of the way as the pallet, closely

Chapter 6 - Welcome to The Madhouse

followed by the forklift truck carrying it, missed me by inches.

"Tipper! Ye fuckin' mad cunt!" Jim bellowed at the driver of the truck who did not even appear to have noticed anything amiss, nor did he react to the tirade of abuse that followed him. He just trundled on, loading his pallet onto the empty train wagon with about as much subtlety as a Panzer Tank driving through the wall of a French Bistro in 1940.

Standing motionless, just my head moving back and forth from the driver to Jim and back again, I waited for this life-threatening incident to be dealt with before my eyes. Expecting Jim to march the driver to the gaffer's office and strip him of his licence etc etc. But no! Nothing! Not a fucking thing happened! Jim just called me over and walked back towards the main road office. Not another thing was said, even though this dickhead 'Tipper' had been a second away from at best seriously injuring me, at worst killing me! Everyone just carried on as if nothing had happened. How naïve I was to the workings of a big factory. As time went on I took the 'near misses' with a pinch of salt.

I walked loose-legged to the office on the road receiving deck; constantly scanning around to make sure no other Kamikaze forklifts had my name written on them. I watched Tipper go back and forth in the same carefree manner from the safety of my new workplace and imagined myself kicking him in the gonads while hitting him with a lump of wood.

Tipper was a career factory worker and was quite literally one of the most stupid people I had ever, have ever, met. He was from a rural area between Redditch and Bromsgrove and looked like your typical banjo-playing throwback. Six feet tall and built like a farmer with fat hay-baling hands, he had shoulder length dark brown curly hair and a face that screamed Neanderthal.

His walk was carried out as if he had a spring under his right foot that pushed him off the floor, throwing his left leg forward to correct. Flicking imaginary hair out of his eyes every ten seconds added a comical effect to his funny walk. The strangest thing was that his voice didn't appear to have broken, even though he was in his early thirties at the time he nearly killed me. He will feature as we progress the tale.

The main office was surrounded by well-worn and battered crash barriers, that had many dents and scratches that supported the reason for their presence. Inside was a computer terminal with a printer, a couple of desks and various chairs scattered around. It was here that I was introduced to Alan who was to become a workmate for the time I was there. He was a friendly thirty-something bloke who loved any sport, and was a Rover Lifer by his own admittance.

"I'll leave ye to it then Al," said Jim as he walked to the door.

"Ok Jim, I'll book this wagon in with him," Alan replied.

At this time the area was full of vehicles and materials and we walked onto the crowded and noisy deck area.

"We'll get through all them today Dave, no problem," Alan indicated to the material scattered all around, "and we might even get Leroy to do some as well."

"Who's Leroy?" I asked.

"Oh, he lives in that little office," Alan pointed to the smaller of the two offices between the loading bay doors.

"I didn't see him when I came in," I stated, puzzled.

"You'll be lucky to see him at all mate, but you'll hear him!" he finished with a smirk.

Chapter 6 - Welcome to The Madhouse

So began my working life at the factory and it didn't take long to pick things up. No sooner had the forklifts dropped the stuff on the ground and back filled with empties, Alan and I had booked it into the computer system, allocating every pallet with a bar coded ticket. Once this was done it was ready to be shipped to the relevant store. It became apparent as the day wore on that every driver who came in brought his paperwork to us, none went to the other smaller office. This I thought was very strange, and I pointed this out to Alan.

"Leroy's on a go-slow because he thinks we are rushing the job" he answered, "most of them know what he's like so they bring the papers here to save any hassle."

"Doesn't Jim say anything to him?" I asked.

"Oh yeah," Alan replied, "regular, but they just end up having a shouting match and nothin' gets sorted. He's quite funny to watch, especially when we get a new driver in who doesn't know him."

Being the inquisitive type, I decided to test Leroy's ferocity and waited for an appropriate candidate. I didn't have to wait long before a 6ft 4 inch mountain of a man walked in, paperwork in hand.

"Can you take your notes over to that office, mate", I indicated towards Leroy's lair.

The driver went a distinct shade of pale.

"You fuckin' jokin' mate?" he replied in a deep Somerset accent.

"No mate," I responded, indicating towards the large pile of papers already on my desk, all the time trying not to smile, but aware of Alan watching in silence and intently over the rim of his tea cup.

With this, the driver turned and walked slowly towards his fate, pausing momentarily, speaking to himself as if rehearsing how he was going to explain this gross interruption of Leroy's time. Then he went in...

"WHAT DE FUCK!...I DON FUCKIN WAN DEM!...FUCK OFF!"

The driver quick-stepped out the office followed by his paperwork which bounced off the crash barrier outside as the office door slammed, rocking the flimsy construction to the core.

All he could do was walk sheepishly back to our office as we desperately tried to compose ourselves.

"Ere, oi think 'e be busy over there, so oi think oi'll wait if that's okay."

"Okay mate," I replied, "just leave them here."

"Oi think oi'm goin' to get a coffee," at which he got up and walked out and I was finally able to release my convulsion.

"You cruel bastard!" Alan laughed.

"I know; I couldn't fukin resist it man!"

"It'll come back on you one day," he warned with a wagging finger.

"I fuckin' hope not!" I finished, laughing, but not imagining how soon I would find myself in a similar situation with the demon that was Leroy.

After about an hour and closing towards the end of shift, Jim walked into the office followed by a 20(ish) year old lad with a chessboard haircut. "This is Russell," said Jim, "he'll be working with you and Alan for the rest of the week."

"Aa bin ya?" came the greeting from Russell who was a Black Country lad."

Now, if Russell was working with Alan..."Davey can you go and work wi' Leroy for a couple of days, mebe that will shut the moanin' bastard up?" Jim left without giving any chance for debate.

I tried not to show my annoyance or concern due to

Chapter 6 - Welcome to The Madhouse

the new face on the team,

"Oh, that's fuckin' great! Fuckin' fan-bastard-tastic!" But failed.

Alan smiled without looking at me, but he didn't have to speak, I knew he was crying with laughter inside.

I picked up my jacket and walked slowly towards the 'Office from Hell'. I had seen Leroy walking to and from the office at the start and end of shifts, and when he needed hot water from the urn. On all these occasions he hadn't even acknowledged my presence. I had heard his tirade of verbal abuse directed at the driver, but had not seen him have a conversation with anyone.

Leroy was a 5ft 7 inch stocky built, light-skinned West Indian in his mid-forties. He had a 'Richard Pryor' afro with matching beard and moustache. His voice was deep and gravely and appeared always to be angry, which he usually was, hence few people argued with him. With the exception of Jim who attempted to 'supervise' him with little or no effect.

I looked into the window of the office and saw that he was reading his paper with his back to me. I looked behind me and saw Bob and Sean (the fork-lift truck drivers) staring in my direction in anticipation. By the other office, Alan and Russell leaned in the doorway, all waiting to see what was going to happen.

I opened the door which creaked to announce my presence.

"Hi ya!"

Silence.

I stepped inside.

"I'm Dave, you've probably seen me across the way, yea?"

Silence...still reading.

"Jim asked me to come and give you a hand."

Silence..... still reading.

"He reckons you've been moanin' about not havin' any help" (nervous laugh by me, followed by silence and continued reading). "Wankaeh?"

Questioning grunt, followed by head movement sharp look in my direction...

"Jim! Jim! I meant Jim..." I clarified with a panicked tone and show of my palms.

Silence, back to paper.

"I'll crack on with this load then, okay?"

Then, in a quiet, deep voice: "You do dat man."

Well, I was to spend the rest of the week with Leroy and that included four hours overtime on the Saturday! We didn't talk much, and we separated at lunch, but we shared cigarettes, made each other drinks and got on with the job, and I suppose we made friends...sort of.

I had settled in well, made friends with other new starters and old hands, and I felt good about myself for the first time in a while. The work was laughable in the area I was in, and after my previous life in retail where I worked like a dog for little reward, this offered me a good work life balance. *I may even get to like it here*, I thought to myself but I knew that this job had a shelf life for me. I picked up my first pay packet at the end of that week and noted I'd doubled my earnings in half the hours. The sun was shining, I was back on the horse and life was good for the first time in a good while.

That was the welcome I had to the 'Madhouse.'

The Bristol Road going South, with the 'Old West Building' on the right. The track going over the road joining the 'West Works' to the rest of the plant.

CHAPTER 7

CULTURE WARS

"Yam a cunt."
[Pretty much every Yam Yam I ever met]

There were workers from all over the UK, Ireland, and internationally employed at the plant during my adventures there. It would be fair to say, and would make geographical sense, that the largest groups were 'Yam Yams' and 'Brummies.' Brummies were the locals from all over the city of Birmingham, and the Yam Yams being from the areas known as the 'Black Country.' The reason for the title "Yam Yam" being applied to the Black Country folk should become apparent shortly.

The Black Country itself is so named due to its industrial history and the fact that the area had a healthy coal seam, a lot of the coal being burnt as industry boomed in the area from the start of the industrial revolution. Purists would suggest that the coal seam itself was the reason for the name. Others would argue it was the amount of soot and ash that was pumped into the air and waterways, covering everything in a coat of blackness.

Now, there were those at the factory of a lower IQ and probably more sinister character, who had little interest in history, who suggested the name came due to the amount of 'fucking Paki's' [People from Pakistan] living in the area. Granted, there was a significant population of people with heritage from South Asia living there. However, no matter how hard you may try to reason with a bigot, facts to them are irrelevant.

One particular fellah decided to offer the fact that the

place was a 'shit hole' hence the name. I rightly pointed out that if this was the case, would it not be the 'Brown, sweet corn speckled Country?' This observation was of course wasted on him.

I would not suggest animosity was the normal state of affairs between these two groups, but it did exist, as human tribalism always pops up somewhere when large groups are thrown together. Local football teams to both areas would even divide those respective groups again. On the whole though, I very rarely saw anything more threatening than the usual 'piss take.'

A major bone of contention for many of us from our respective areas being discussed is the continual misrepresentation of our dialects. I am not sure how many times I have been close to throwing something at the TV when an 'actor' playing the part of a Brummie, sets about using what is clearly a Black Country dialect or vice versa. Even worse when the two are just thrown together! This has been set to rights in no small measure by my namesake who directed the series 'Peaky Blinders.' The actor 'Paul Anderson' pretty much nailed the brummie speak, which is of great credit to him. Especially so since he was hamstrung by originating from London, where they really do speak funny.

Irrespective of all this previous information, and please feel free to delve deeper into the history of Birmingham and the Black Country, I feel it is incumbent upon me to offer some guidance into the respective differences of the dialects. Hopefully this information will give you a better handle of the conversations that take place within this read, and offer a guide should you feel the need to visit these areas. So, here is a brief guide to the types Brummie and Yam Yam grammar that I have been exposed to.

Chapter 7 - Culture Wars

Black Country;

Yam: You, [source of the nickname]

Yem: You

Yama: You are

Yema: You are

Aya: Aren't you

Amya: Are you

Abinya: How are you

Ayit: Isnt it. i.e., "That ayit". Can also be used as a positive confirmation.

Itay: It isn't

Day: Didn't. i.e. "I day do it"

War: Wasn't

Warit: Wasn't it. i.e. "that war it"

Buzz: Bus

Curryarse: Nope! Nothing to do with the after effects of a spicy meal, but in fact refers to the location where you will purchase the spicy meal.

Clacker: Retention muscles in the anus, or the anus as a whole; i.e. 'Kick in the clacker'.

Bonk: Bank. Or can be used to describe the act of sex.

Merry Hill: An enormous shopping centre/mall where Yam Yam's congregate to spend their cash on shit they don't need.

Fudge Packer: A member of the male gay community.

Split Arse: A woman.

Faggots and pays: A local delicacy. Faggots being a ball of 'meat' in gravy, served with fat peas that are mashed. Known as 'mushy pays'.

Yamacunt: You are a cunt. This can be expressed as 'Yemacunt'. Very important this one, so please take note. Being called a cunt in some cultures can be deemed as quite offensive and may lead to considerable offence. However, this is not necessarily the case in Black Country interactions. It can be directed at you in many situations including;
- When you tell a funny joke or story that causes laughter and joviality.
- When you tell a poor joke or story that causes groans or eye roll.
- If you make a tit out of yourself or have an accident.
- If you offer a stupid comment to a conversation.

Possibly the only time you should show concern would be when the Yam Yam delivering the comment appears to be in a state of agitation or anger. For instance, if you are in a boozer and this comment is directed at you. Note if the Yam Yam is standing with a defensive gait, and is holding his pint glass tightly. This may signal an opportune moment to leave. If the subject has any liquid left in their pint glass, you have time to make an exit, as no self respecting Yam Yam would waste perfectly good beer.

Dropping the 'C' bomb has less and less impact in our more modern times, not dissimilar to the liberation of 'Fuck' and it's now common everyday use. I personally like to save it for those special occasions when no other word quite encapsulates how I am feeling about a person or a situation. Let us take the occasions when I have hit my little toe on the corner of the table leg or popped my finger with a hammer. I find the ejaculation of the C bomb into the atmosphere really does help with the pain. I would best describe it as a grammatical paracetamol.

There are many phrases and words that could be

Chapter 7 - Culture Wars

added to the list, however they would be claimed by both camps, and I don't want to start an international incident.

Brummie;

It may be important to note, when attempting to use the below words and phrases, that Brummies have a tendency to roll their 'r' when speaking. Takes years of practice so don't stress. Also of note, as you may or may not have heard, the Brummie dialect is one of the least favourite amongst Brits. Take no notice, they are talking bollox! Most of the bad press is put down to the usual North/South divide and social snobbery. In fact, according to studies from the uni of Birmingham, foreigners actually like the Brummie twang! So stick that in your pipe!

Yow: You [Could be claimed by both camps, but we are having that one].

Ya: You

Brummie: A person from Birmingham, England

Brum: Birmingham

Brummagen: The Birmingham dialect

Brummie Screwdriver: A hammer: Also referred to as the Brummagen Screwdriver.

Oroight: Alright. A greeting. Not to be taken as a question enquiring about your mental state.

Fuckin': Fucking. [Obvious, but I thought it would help my proof reader].

Bostin: Something or an experience that is really good.

Bab: A friendly term used to refer to another person, especially children but not limited to them.ie, "Oroight bab".

Gooin: Going.

Luv, Luva: Love. Used in general conversation when

speaking to a member of the opposite sex. Especially useful when you can't remember their name.

Fag: Cigarette.

Boozer: A public house or a person who drinks too much alcohol.

Outdoor: Bottle Shop, place to purchase alcohol

Cob: Bread Roll

Pop: A carbonated soft drink

Yampy: Not the full shilling, one can short of a six pack. [Make sense?]

Muffdiva: One who partakes of the joys of oral sex on a female. Can be used as a term to describe a gay female.

Mucka: Work mate or friend.

Waratit: Reference to a stupid person.

Shit my tits off: A term used to express dismay or disbelief, not limited.

Carl Fuckin'Chinn: Carl Chinn, Brummie historian [I am not bitter!] For a more concise view of Birmingham life and grammar, I would happily endorse the 'Brummagen' magazine by Carl Fuckin' Chinn. Unlike Carl, who wouldn't endorse my book.

I am not bitter!

CHAPTER 8

THE CORNER SHOP

"The sale or supply of unauthorised goods or services is prohibited within the confines of Rover Group premises."
[A dusty sign]

As time went on and the opportunity arose, similar to when the company computer system would crash for unknown reasons and sometimes employee based reasons, occasionally deliberate, I would wander around familiarising myself with my surroundings. It became very apparent that you could purchase just about anything if you knew who to talk to and where to look.

"Any chance I could nip over the shop and get some fags, Jim?" I asked, sucking on the last smoke I had in the box.

"Why don't you get them from Tel? He replied with a knowing movement of his head in the direction of the track area.

I looked at him with obvious puzzlement and he clarified,

"Just see Gary and he'll point ye in the right direction." Jim pointed at a train driver standing at the top of the deck.

Gary walked me along gangways, up metal stairs and through workstations until we came to a group of about ten blokes who were busy welding, bolting and screwing bits of metal onto bigger bits of metal that were travelling along the conveyor next to them.

"Oroight, Gaz?" said a middle-aged man appearing from the huddle.

"Hi ya Tel, got a new customer for ya. This is Dave." Gary nodded his head in my direction.

"Oroight, Dave? Just started have ya?"

"Yeah, couple of weeks ago. I'm told you flog fags?" I enquired.

"Arr, what yafta?"

"What ya got?" I replied with surprise expecting to see a box of 200 appear of one brand. At this, Tel proceeded to open a folding case. I'm sure you know the sort, like those doctors have with lots of little shelves and drawers? Inside was an assortment of every type of tobacco you could name. A positively wonderous array of coloured boxes and tobacco pouches to entice even the most discerning addict. In fact, a better display in a supermarket kiosk you would be unlikely to find.

"Change a twenty, Tel?" I asked knowing full well what the answer would be.

At this, he opened another drawer loaded with paper money and coins neatly laid out like a shop till. He handed me my smokes and the change to my twenty pound note with a smile.

"Okay kidda, see ya again." This was a hint, I think, as a small queue of regulars had appeared behind me.

I noticed as we left "Tel's Tobacconist" that we were not going back the way we came.

"Shouldn't we be going this way, Gaz?"

"Oh yeah, sorry mate, I was just goin' to see Pete the Hat on the way back."

"Pete the Hat?" I asked.

"Yeah, shoes, trainers, clothing, you know what I mean?"

"Oh yeah, fair enough." I didn't know.

We wandered towards the rectification area, which, if the company motto of 'RIGHT FIRST TIME' was to be

Chapter 8 - The Corner Shop

believed, shouldn't have existed? As it was, it was full of car bodies waiting to be rectified. I digress...

We approached an area, which was completely screened off with thick black curtains, and standing in the middle of a number of welding machines was a chap with a white flat cap on. *Pete the Hat*, I assumed.

Pete was a middle-aged man with shoulder length black curly hair which was full and thick all around his neck and ears. His 'Job' involved welding things together in between running the Longbridge general clothing store.

"Oroight, Pete?" greeted Gaz.

"How ya doin, Gaz?" was the reply from Pete, confirming my assumption.

"What ya got in?" Gaz continued.

"'Eya, come round and ave a look," at which Pete walked into another thickly curtained area which protected passers-by from sparks from the welders. He fiddled with a padlock on a 7ft tall, 6ft wide metal cabinet, stepping back as he opened the substantial doors. Inside were lines and lines of running shoes, all neatly stacked on top of each other with a display pair on top of each box. All the top names were present in all styles and colours.

Gary selected a pair of size 9's keeping his feet on the cardboard flooring in place so as not to get them dirty if he decided not to make a purchase.

"Got 'em in a 9½, Pete?"

"Ye want a kick in the bollocks, Gary?"

Both smiled at each other.

"35 quid to you Gary."

"I'll give ya 30 coz of the mark eya." Gary pointed to a black scuff mark about the size of an atomic molecule on the heel of one of the running shoes.

"Ye tight-arse fucker! I bet you can peel a Satsuma in ye pocket! No! 35 quid or put them back!" Pete pretended to be angry.

"Ooooooooo!" said Gary sarcastically, "okay, I'll take 'em."

"Do you want anythin', Dave?" Pete looked at me and indicated to his display.

"Nah, I'm okay for shoes, got any jeans or shirts or shit like that?"

Pete smiled and walked to a row of tall, slim metal lockers, opening them all to reveal a huge selection of jeans, t-shirts, polo shirts and all manner of other tops.

"Bugger me!" I said in surprise.

"No thanks son, we only take cash" at which Pete burst into a fit of laughter at his own joke. So much so that his hat fell off as he slumped in his rest time chair.

With his hat missing, a completely hairless scalp was revealed in complete contrast to the thick locks on show below his cap. Needless to say, Gary and I found this just as amusing and joined in with the belly laughter.

After we had finished our childish guffawing and Pete had replaced his hat, I purchased some goods. It was at this point that I noted I was not in possession of funds to pay for the items I had selected.

"Don't worry son" Pete reassured with a huge smile, "You can have an account and pay weekly."

Further surprised by the availability of a credit account I joked "Oh and what happens if I forget to pay!"

Calmly but with a hint of a sinister tone Pete replied "I'll fukin' kill ya."

I laughed out loud and looked at Gary to try and make light, but Gary's face was not showing any humour.

"Oh shit!" I said as I looked at my watch and realised that our five-minute break had turned into half an hour!

"What's up?" Gary asked.

"Jimbo's gonna do his fruit! Look at how long we've

Chapter 8 - The Corner Shop

been gone! Thanks Pete, lovely to meet ya, I'll get that money to ya by Friday, come on then Gary" I rushed Gary to the aisle.

"Fuckin' Hell, Dave. Ya can tell you're new!" Gary chuckled.

"What ya mean?" I asked.

"Just don't worry. Thompson won't give a shit where yev been and as long as you pay Pete on time he won't kill ya."

He was right, Jim didn't give a shit and Pete never killed me once. I realised that after such strict working conditions in my previous life, I had entered a world where as long as the job gets done, no one gave a shit where you were.

As the weeks and months went on, my excursions off to other parts of the plant increased, and if any comment was made about my absence, I would say "I was lookin' for a part" or "I was in the shithouse." 99% of the time, no one asked, and if you give me an inch.

One of the other services provided by members of the workforce was gambling. You could put money on just about any race, falling just short of having our own bookies! Unfortunately, so word had it, those that ran the service did not tell the tax man, who subsequently investigated and closed the operation down. Someone told me the incident was in the local paper and that it was estimated that the annual turnover was around £300,000! Of course, management denied all knowledge of this disgraceful operation, but I'm sure many betting slips were disposed of in a hurry on the day the taxman came.

Prior to the lottery, the football pools was the quickest way for the common man to become a millionaire, and it is fair to say that many of my work mates spent large amounts of money on a Friday in anticipation of 'winning the big one' on a Saturday. Of course, we had our own collector 'John' who used to wander around the plant on a Thursday and Friday collecting money.

John had a clip-board that he carried absolutely everywhere. However, in the five years I knew him, I never saw him write anything on it, or even have any documentation other than the same tatty pieces of headed company paper that just got dirtier as time went on. I asked people what he did, but no one knew, nor did anyone see him doing anything that remotely looked like a work-related activity. There was a theory that he didn't even work for the firm, he just had company coveralls and wandered in one day to corner the market.

Amusingly, he had huge sags in his coveralls where his pockets were due to the amount of coins he carried and collected. I once saw him with empty pockets, which looked like saddlebags due to the regular stress they were put under. Walking around with 15 kilo's in coins on each leg would give him legs like a sprinter, I thought. I once commented "I bet ya could run 100 metres in 10 seconds with ya trousers off, eh John?"

"Don't be such a cunt" he replied.

Home entertainment was another area covered by some workers, and you could buy computers, TVs, videos, stereos and other like goods, still in the box and with a guarantee! I use the word guarantee loosely of course, and the usual course for an unsatisfied customer was to throw the item at the seller and get into a punch up. Where they came from is anyone's guess, but I never purchased anything to find out. [Honest!] Compact Discs (copies of course) and video cassettes made by Black Beard were available with all the latest titles.

We also had a video rental shop run by Ray and his mate Dave. All the latest films were available at half

Chapter 8 - The Corner Shop

the normal price to rent. I rented from Ray on a few occasions and never once understood a word he said due to his broad Black Country dialect and the surrounding noise. He would shout in my direction and I would just nod my head and give him the thumbs up. Dave would give me the correct translation on request.

Fresh food was available such as pre-packed meat, eggs and other various dairy products, but I was a little more cautious about these goods. I mean, if your TV or Video blows up then you buy another or try and get your money back. If you buy a faulty pack of bacon, at best you might end up on the toilet for a couple of days, at worst you could end up in the local mortuary!

Fred, the egg man, always believed in trying new methods of sales banter to improve his sales. He would tell people they were 'Free Range' or 'Barn Eggs', anything to improve his profits. He once told a bloke who had questioned as to why they were so cheap, and was told it was due to the fact they 'fell off the back of a lorry'. Not the most convincing argument, eh?

You could get 200 cigarettes off the lorry drivers for less than half the normal price, but you were not always sure what it was you were actually smoking. All a bit shady! I'm sure all these unnecessary purchases could be avoided if we had people in power that saw just how much was coming in and reduced the duty so it wasn't worth the smugglers doing it on a regular basis. However, I'm sure they have our best interests at heart when they put the duty up so we can't afford to buy them. [blah blah]

Ironically, the only thing I couldn't get at a reduced price were car parts and accessories! I once tried to buy bits for Tracy's Mini 1000 thinking that my 'Rover discount' would save me pounds. Quite the opposite, even with my discount they were 50% more expensive than the local universal car spares shop. Needless to say, some saw the opportunity to make a few quid in this area, and I heard many stories of large quantities of stereos, wheels, tyres, engines and whole vehicles (not yet registered) making their way out through the gates.

If there can be a funny side to theft, then it would be the day that Les the security guard got a brand new van:

"Six miles on the clock it's got!" he stated, proudly to anyone who would listen.

The very next morning as I walked towards the New West Building, on the road outside I saw Les standing beside his new van looking very glum.

"Mornin' Les!" I greeted.

"Can't fuckin' believe it!" he said in a saddened manner.

"What's up mate?" I asked.

"Ave a look." He indicated to the rear of his pride and joy and I noted the absence of both the rear doors.

"Fuck me, Les! What's happened?" said I as I desperately tried to subdue my smirk.

"Twelve miles it's got on the clock, and some twat has nicked the doors. Not the stereo mind, just the fuckin' doors!"

I walked off slowly, trying to show as much sympathy as I could, but failing miserably.

It may come as a surprise to some, that even though the company was a multimillion dollar affair and would naturally be a clear target for the criminal fraternity, its security arrangements, in my opinion, left a great deal to be desired.

I mean no offence to the individuals who were employed to 'guard' the factory and all its assets, but conversations relating to rates of pay amongst them,

Chapter 8 - The Corner Shop

would suggest that you were not going to get the most motivated guardians.

These souls were few and far between, and even though all the gates were supposed to be covered, you could pretty much wander in and out of the place 24 hours a day, 7 days a week unhindered. I even took the liberty on a few occasions at the weekend during overtime shifts, to drive my own car in, to save the walk from the car park.

In addition to the usual replenishment of domestic toilet paper and cleaning material if one of the cleaners forgot to lock their store room, and the abundance of gardening gloves, this situation allowed for the most brazen of thefts. One in particular comes to mind from my time in the old west part of the factory.

Situated throughout the factory were vending machines offering the usual healthy, full sugar snacks and drinks. All of these machines were cash only. I would regularly visit the old west machine during the shift gap between 4.30pm and the start of the night shift at 8.30pm for a fix, while this part of the factory was devoid of production personnel but stores still arriving. On a few occasions the cash box would be missing after being forcibly removed and the signs would state 'out of order'.

On this particular occasion the whole machine had gone. I asked one of the security lads, who worked at the main gate nearby, where the machine had gone. I was surprised [or maybe not] to hear that 'someone' had nicked the whole fucking machine!

Amazed? Well don't be, that was the very tip of the iceberg. In my latter career I was privy to information that would make your mouth drop open in an involuntary manner as to the extent of the theft that went on and the guile of the thieves. I will of course not offer detail as I do not want to be picked up by the UK old bill for some illegal disclosure or somethin'.

Have no doubt that anything could be had if you wanted it, someone always knew someone who knew someone. In fact Saddam Hussain himself might have saved himself a lot of trouble getting the bits for his 'superguns' or a little depleted uranium if he had known someone who worked at the factory.

CHAPTER 9

THE NIGHT SHIFT

"I love nights, it's like havin' a week off."
[The general consensus amongst Logistics staff]

"So, there I was, in ma jeep, two miles from the North Korean border. I'd been promoted to Staff Sgt and was doin' a reccy of forward obs points. The Nips were only a mile or so away and I could hear the enemy guns."

Jim sipped a little of his tea and I noted his eyes scanning from side to side - his mind ticking over as he went back to his story.

"All of a sudden, an eleven tonner came over the brow of the hill and screeched to a halt right next to our jeep. It was full of injured squaddies from the front."

"Thank God you're here, Jim" came a voice from the front passenger, and I looked up to see Montgomery himself..."

"Oh, fuck off, Jim" Alan exclaimed.

"Quiet you, you're too young to even remember the Korean War!" Jim retaliated.

"Was Montgomery in Korea?" I asked quizzically and with a hint of sarcasm.

"Of course he was! Look, de ye want to hear this story or not?" asked Jim, becoming increasingly agitated.

"The emphasis on story you bull-shitting sweaty sock!" replied Alan.

"Watch ye sel' son, I'm a black belt and that's fighting talk!" Jim took a 'Bruce Lee' stance.

"What's an eleven tonner?" adds Russell.

"It's an army lorry," I informed him.

"Anyway..." Jim pipes up again.

"...What's up, Monty?" I ask, and noticed that he was in a terrible state.

"Who's Monty?" interrupts Russell,

"Oh, ye thick fuckin' Yam Yam! I'm wastin' mah time and fuckin' breath!", Jim tried to look exasperated.

"Who am ye callin' a Yam Yam?"

"Davey, I need a quick word", Jim walked out of the office showing me a beckoning finger, and I followed him. "I need ye to do me a favour Davey, we're a bit short on nights, so I'd like ye to cover for a week."

Up to this point, I had been working day shifts which suited me and others as opposed to those who worked nights. In fact I had never worked a night shift before so I looked forward to the chance of experiencing a new change in life style (yeah, right!).

"How long's a week, Jim?" I asked knowing that a week can mean a month in a big organisation.

"Oh, just the one until we get permanent cover" Jim reassured me. "I'm just goin' down to recruit someone from the Old West. Come down an al tell ye the rest of ma story."

We walked slowly and picked up a machine coffee on the way as Jim told me how he had told Monty to "calm down an' pull ye'sel' together!" and went on to organise an orderly withdrawal and regroup. What a fuckin' hero!

The Old West Receiving Office was manned (can I say that?) by factory lifers who had been in the job many many years, stuck in their ways and not enjoying the company's newfound theory of movement of labour and flexibility. Norman had been in the Old West for 20 years or more and was not overly pleased about Jim's request:

"No, no, no, no, I'm not doin' it. NO!" he shouted, banging his hand on the desktop.

Chapter 9 - The Night Shift

"Look! Ye'll do as you're told!" Jim put his "in charge" head on. "I want you in the New West at Eight-Thirty-Five PM on Monday. That's that!"

"No! No! No! No! I won't!"

"Yer will, or yer will go an see Callaghan and tell him why!" (Jim Callaghan was the logistics manager).

"A-HA! He already knows why", Norman looked very self-assured.

"Oh, and pray tell WHAT reason did ye give him?"

"Medical reasons," Norman retorted, sounding very matter-of-fact.

"Go on..." Jim pushed.

"I'm a schizophrenic on medication!"

"Well, that's no reason not to work different shifts." Jim responded with an air of knowing about these things in his voice.

"Yeah? And how do you work that out Dr fuckin' sweaty sock Kildare!?" Norman looked around at his colleagues, nodding and smiling as if to seek praise for his witty rebuke.

"Simple. Stop taking the tablets, then one of you can work days, and the other you can work nights!" Jim replied with an air of obviousness about him.

I snorted a large quantity of coffee through my nose as Jim's comment hit home. Norman sat with a bright red face and Jim turned and walked out the office without a further comment or hint of emotion, leaving me smiling insanely at all present. I walked out quickly to find Jim with a cheery grin on his face.

"Fuckin' Schizophrenic? My arsehole!"

Monday night, 8:35pm and I arrived to be greeted by the night foreman, Bernard Frost or 'Frosty' as he was known. He was a 6ft 4 inch stocky built middle-aged man with a HUGE pot belly, square glasses and a stern demeanour. Oh yeah! He also had 'Lego' hair, you know, as if he put it on out of a box in the morning!

"Thanks for comin', son." He said staring down at me.

"No problem." I replied a little pensively.

Walking into the office with a totally new crew was like starting on my first day all over again, but with a difference. The day shift had many new starters who were in the same boat as me, and the whole make up of the workers seemed younger and more sociable. The night crew were long term employees, like Norman (schizo'), and very suspicious and stuck in their ways. They enjoyed routines and stuck to them rigidly. Unlike during the day time, every load arrived at fixed times as did the trains coming in and out. Break times were rigid and the workers had designed methods of work and nothing changed. Everyone knew their job and did it in the same way every day.

Ken and Alf made up the road crew, while Derek and Geoff were the rail receivers, with assorted strange-looking 'too long doing night shift' forklift truck drivers. All were sat in the office sipping the pre-shift cuppa when I arrived for my shift.

"How ya doin' lads?" was my opening greeting which was met by a quiet mumble and grunts from the group.

"Hmmmm...sociable lot," I thought to myself.

I attempted to become a part of the team to no avail. Ken and Alf began together and as much as they stated they didn't care what I did as long as the work was done, I could tell that they didn't welcome any interference.

"Fuck 'em" I thought, and off I went to Leroy's hut [devoid of Leroy of course) and did my own thing. Break time came and I went over to the main office to make myself a drink. To my utter amazement, a hot cup of tea was sat on the table waiting for me!

"I've not put sugar in it," said Alf.

"No, that's fine...Thanks!" my 'anti' attitude was immediately knocked off balance and I thought it was only proper to remain with them and share the break time in their company. With that, the conversation around me began and I was included without prejudice.

Derek and Geoff were a double act even though they didn't realise it. Derek was a 60-something whining Brummie, and Geoff was a 60-something loud Yam Yam. They didn't speak to each other, just shouted insults in between speaking to others present.

Alf was within six months of retirement and was counting every minute, whereas Ken younger but still middle-aged. Something I found very amusing as the week went on was the way Geoff, Derek and Alf spoke to and treated Ken. Due to the twenty-year age gap, Ken was seen as the young apprentice and was referred to as 'young fella' and 'sunshine'. "Go and put the kettle on, there's a good lad." I heard Derek say to him on more than one occasion. I was young enough at twenty-four to be Ken's son, but I was treated as one of the blokes and called 'Dave', full stop. Ken didn't bat an eyelid and seemed to enjoy it. Middle age crisis perhaps?

I sipped my tea and smiled at the insulting one-liners thrown from Derek to Geoff and back again. The room eventually returned to silence.

"Dave, can you book this pallet of hinges in? They need them on the track pronto." Frosty's question was a directive, and I lifted myself up without a thought to comply with the request.

"Sit Down!" I braced as Alf put his hand out indicating that I should stay in my seat.

"We are on our break. We have six minutes left." He

finished and I looked back in the direction of Frosty.

"They need them before the track starts up." Frosty shouted with obvious agitation.

"Tough!" said Geoff, "They should've got 'em earlier. We ay doin' nothin' durin' break time, so Fuck off!"

"Dave, just book 'em in and take no notice of these old farts", continued Frosty.

"Don't you dare! Take no notice of that fuckin' Bully!" added Derek, pointing at Frosty.

"Look! We need that part now! So stop being so fuckin' pedantic and let Dave book it in!" a bead of sweat ran down Frosty's increasingly reddening face.

"Ooooooooooooh, swallowed a fuckin' dictionary?" asked Alf, sarcastically.

"No. I just learned to read and write at school you fuckin' thick mong!"

"Cheeky Bastard!" Alf looked genuinely a little hurt.

"You want to be careful not to be so hurtful, yem can cause people long term damage coming out with comments like that!" Geoff offered concern to the exchange.

"Oh, hark at Oprah Winfrey over there!" said Frosty, exasperated.

"Who the fuck is Oprah Winfrey?" enquired Derek.

"Look!" Frosty raised his hands as if to call a truce, "if we don't get that part to the track now it will stop and every minute lost costs us £10,000, right!"

"If I've told you once, I've told you a million times, don't exaggerate!" Derek giggled childishly, looking around for support.

"Why do you always crack the same shit joke you stupid Brummie Twat?" Geoff asked.

"Will you Pleeeeeeeeese book this part in?" shouted Frosty in a desperate tone, and almost simultaneously the

Chapter 9 - The Night Shift

roar of the factory began as the break ended.

Alf jumped up and with one swoop of his light pen the part was booked and the paperwork stamped.

"Tea Break over lads," he smiled slyly as Frosty walked away looking thoroughly agitated.

"Keeps 'em on their toes" Alf whispered to me.

"Let the fuckers know who's boss!" added Derek.

"Shut up you cunt," snorted Geoff and they wandered off towards the rail receiving deck shouting inaudible comments at each other as they walked.

"Come on young man, let's get cracking," Alf beckoned to Ken and at one point I thought he was going to hold out his hand for him to hold. Ken hopped up and I'm sure he skipped at one point on his way to the door.

This was my first experience of worker power and I realised that, regardless of who was in charge or what title he/she may have had, it was the lowly graded employee that held the power in their hands. If the theory was correct and we built a car an hour, then every minute lost was the price of a car. Of course, you have to be selling them too, but if the workers didn't like what was going on, then it stopped! ...And that was that!

Mid-week came and I began to realise how different the volume of work was on a night. We had probably half as much to do which, needless to say, led to my wandering around in order to avoid boredom setting in. Frosty gave me the chance to spread my wings to the other side of the plant to collect some items from the stores. He gave me directions and I decided to walk rather than use a ferry car.

I walked up to Q Gate which is probably the most visible part of the plant, and is usually where reports on the news came from. In I walked, and to this day I have no idea how I got to where I needed to be, nor could I find it again. I walked through parts of the plant in total darkness compared to the other areas buzzing with life in the sheer light.

One area I came upon appeared to be a large store area for foam and seat-type material. I had met a security guard by this time that was walking with me as 'it was on his rounds'. He was a strange chap, weird eyed and clingy, and full of stories about different parts of the factory being haunted.

"What's that noise?" I whispered and as I listened into the darkness I could hear grunting and snoring coming from a large pile of foam squares piled high in one corner of the room. I then became aware of similar sleepy noise coming from other locations elsewhere in the room.

"Shhhhhh!" said my new travelling companion, "don't wake them up or they'll have the Union on ya!"

"What? Who are you talking about?" I whispered in response.

"I think they do somemink wiv seats an' shit, but they're on piece-work and they musta finished for the week."

It was the early hours of Wednesday morning, and bearing in mind the working week for nights was 8:35pm to 7:00am for four nights only, how could they have finished for the week, whoever 'they' were. In addition, I was under the impression that 'piece-work' had gone long ago and you worked until you were told to stop. Obviously not!

I heard a loud snoring noise coming from another direction and began to make out shapes sleeping in the foam piles. "Cheeky bastards!" I thought, and decided to give them an early morning wake-up call. I walked over to the gangway leading out and saw that the Main light switches has been levered to 'OFF'. Not for long.

Chapter 9 - The Night Shift

With one jerk, 'ON' it went causing twenty thousand 2 metre long fluorescent tubes to hum into action, slowly illuminating the area as if it were midday in summer.

"Oh shit! What ya do that for?"

My companion panicked and nearly knocked me over heading for the door. I followed him and could hear the angry shouts behind me. I paused momentarily and, like a scene from Michael Jackson's 'Thriller', bodies started climbing out of their sleepy foam graves.

Outside, I chuckled to myself.

"Ya shouldn't a done that ye know mate."

"Fuck 'em!" I responded with a hint of venom, which was uncalled for, "If I've got to stay up, so can they!"

We continued on our way with more ghost stories from my companion about dead factory employees haunting the very same places they used to work.

"I've seen at least two ye know, like a gloomy glowin' thing, not touchin' the floor. Scared me shitless!" my 'friend' was becoming stranger by the minute, so I decided to part company with him.

"Yeah, anyway, thanks for the company, best I be getting' back." I made my excuses and quickened my pace, leaving him behind.

"Ten years of nights I've 'ad ya know, and I've seen 'em..." his voice echoed behind me and I saw his face light up as he placed his torch under his chin, then switched it off, then on again, then off again. Clearly taking the piss.

"Fuckin' weirdo!" I thought and my pace quickened to a slow jog.

I was glad to be back on the deck in its daylight conditions after my little jaunt, loaded with pens, Tippex, paper and other bits.

"Where the fuck have you been?" Frosty asked trying to sound as if he was bothered, "I was just about to send out a search party!"

"I got a bit lost, that's all," I lied.

"Did you see any hassle over there? Apparently the line stopped for 15 minutes cos someone upset the upholsterers!"

"NO, No, nothing...saw nothing."

On my last night I met Les for the first time, and it was one of those moments when you realise you have met someone very special. Les was a West Indian, coming over to 'HINGLAND' in the fifties to find work with many of his brothers and sisters. He was a devout Christian, loving the singing, dancing and praying that came with his church life. He was one of the night crew through and through, in his sixties but built like a 20 year old athlete with an old man's head. He worked with me on the road receiving area and was an absolute joy. We talked about all sorts of things and he told me stories about his young life. Not once did he curse or say anything negative and his influence rubbed off on me, if only for a short time.

His temperament was tested by all around who would tease him light heartedly, especially at break-time when Geoff and Derek got together.

"Ya feelin' better, Les?" Alf enquired as Les had been off sick for 3 days.

"Oh yes, tank you, I ham feelin' much better now."

"What was up we ya?" probed Derek.

"Jus feelin' a bit run down, ya know how it is when you get te our age?"

"Ya know what that is, Les?" Geoff remarked and shuffled in his chair, shaking his paper out straight then focusing on it. (*Here it comes*, I thought).

"Yes, I think it was flu," Les informed him.

"No, no..." Geoff went on, "...too much shaggin' that's why yem under the weather an weak!"

"Oh, God forgive you!" Les shouted raising his hands and flapping them in Geoff's direction.

"No, straight up, Les," Geoff looked at Les as he placed his paper on the desk.

"No! Shut up! Shut up! You bad man!" Les put his hands over his ears.

"No, listen, it's a well known fact that white women in their sixties are just not interested in sex, but those Big Mamas like your missus Les, well they just can't get enough, can they?" It wasn't clear if this was a question or a statement of fact.

"Stop now Geoff, that is bad talk," Les attempted to ignore Geoff by picking up a magazine off the table, then putting it down quickly as he realised it was a copy of "Penthouse".

"Look..." Geoff persisted, "Are ya tellin' me that Les has got arms like a fuckin' gymnast from workin' 'ere?" He paused as he placed the evidence in front of us. "Of course not, it's from liftin' that great big weight up and down of ye cock, en it Les?" at which the room erupted into fits of laughter, and Les walked over to the teapot to pour another drink. He had his back to us but the movement of his shoulders betrayed his laughter.

"I can't remember the last time I did!" said Alf, glumly causing the mood to shift, "I mean, when I met my wife we went at it all the time, any time."

"Certainty kills the sex drive," Ken added.

"What does?" asked Alf.

"Weddin' cake!" which lifted the mood back up again.

"In de beginin' God created de earth, den rested..." Les began his sermon, "then he created man, and rested..."

"HALLELUJAH!" shouted Geoff.

"...then he created woman...and man has not rested

since!" again the room erupted and Les laughed the loudest, clicking his fingers from the wrist.

I was quite sad to go back onto days after the week came to an end. I had had an unexpectedly good time and fitted in well, enjoying the company and the very base sense of humour. But this was not to be my last contact with the night crew; it was to be the first of many.

CHAPTER 10

MEET THE LADIES

"I aye a sexist,
yem will never hear me swear in front of a split arse."
[Shall remain nameless]

To say that sexism and general male bias within the factory was the norm would be the biggest understatement since Edwina Curry MP, said to her PR managers prior to her famous 'Egg Speech' and subsequent UK egg market collapse, "Who the fuck am I going to upset talking about eggs?" Men appeared to make up about 99.99% of the workforce so it followed that the few women who braved that statistic got a lot of attention.

Men are very strange animals. I mean, you take a bloke leaving home, kissing his lovely partner goodbye, and when he arrives in his male-dominated world he becomes a different person. Any female would immediately become the target of lewd comments and sexual grunts and gesticulation. The irony of much of this is that the female could have a face like a bulldog licking piss off a thistle, as many of them did. However in the high-testosterone male dominated areas of the factory she became a goddess. Some blokes had girlfriends and partners who were absolute stunners, but even they would get wound up over the most ordinary looking female employee.

The ladies worked away from the heavy work areas and usually ended up on light machinery with a few exceptions. Many took advantage of their sex and found a niche somewhere carrying a clipboard looking for parts or shadowing a gaffer.

Living in a Plant

This was the case in the West Works, but across the plant they filled many roles that were 'done by the women' as well as matching their male counterparts in given areas deemed 'for the blokes'.

Angela was a girl blessed with a huge smile and a couple of other interestingly sized assets. She could have been described as an attractive girl outside the factory by those who found her appealing, but inside the factory she was without equal. She would wander through the factory with her friend, Lisa, who was an ordinary 30-something without a personality and not much to look at. They would be followed by the usual barrage of lewd comments as they went about their buisness. If they stopped at a coffee machine, a queue would form ready to light her fag and buy her drink. She had the look that said "Yeah, shout all your comments, but touch me and I'll rip your fuckin' balls off," and no-one ever did.

One particular female employee, who will remain nameless, took her status a tad too far in my opinion. While making my way to a toilet block on a first floor level overlooking the 5th Aisle Stores I had to pass a locker area which serviced a large amount of production line workers. The plant was running so the locker room was empty, or should've been. As I passed I heard a subtle rattle and banging noise coming from within the labyrinth. Curiosity got the better of me so I went to investigate and began to hear the noise of heavy male breathing.

In the far corner I could see two bodies standing very close together, one with its back to another and it was at this point that I perceived two men 'at work'. This was primarily due to the fact that both looked male. I felt that it would be inappropriate to be caught watching, and probably worse than taking part! Problem was, I decided to have a closer look in order to identify the

Chapter 10 - Meet the Ladies

parties for future gossip due to the unusual circumstances (old woman, eh?). This was to be my downfall. As I edged forward I pushed two lockers together resulting in a loud bang which alerted the couple to my presence.

Both looked back and, to my surprise (and relief), it was the aforementioned female who was on the receiving end of an as yet unidentified male's amorous advances.

"Do you fuckin' mind?" asked the male voice.

Oh, that's rich, seeing as though you've got your cock up her arse and I might want to get into that locker you're leaning on! I thought. Instead I replied, "Yeah, no, sorry," and walked off noting that they had resumed without a thought. I saw our locker room loving girl on numerous occasions and she never bat an eyelid, in fact I think I was more embarrassed than she was!

Even within the male domain there were areas where the ladies were in the majority and ruled the roost. One particular area that would test the resilience of any bloke was the sewing rooms where they made the seat covers and linings.

I had the misfortune to pass through this area on my way somewhere or other after a few months in the job. I was with Barry, a fellow starter who had just joined us on the deck. Barry was in his late twenties and could be described as a handsome, dumb blonde from the Black Country.

"We'll take a short-cut through the sewing room, Barry." I instructed.

"Oooh, I've heard about that place - fellahs goo in an' day doo'come out!"

"Bollocks!" I replied, subtle as ever, "what could a bunch of women possibly do to worry us?" My naivety at such a young age was startling.

As we entered the room, the noise from the machines

Living in a Plant

hit my ears. Barry walked quickly and I slowed him to a more suitably time-wasting pace by grabbing his arm.

"That yer boyfriend, Luv?" the squawk from behind was followed by female laughter and mixed with "oohs" and "aahs".

I looked around and noticed that we were now the centre of attention after just 30 feet of intrusion into the she-bitch domain!

"Mind you, I can't blame him, he's a luvly looking' fellah!" came the same voice again and I smiled at the various faces in a sarcastic manner.

Young, old, fat, thin, pretty, pretty ugly and positively grotesque women of all ages filled the room. A well-endowed, aesthetically-deprived individual blocked our way with her bulk and her attention was fixed on poor Barry, who had begun to sweat and looked flushed.

"Hello, dahlin', what's yer name?" said chubby (well, you don't expect me to keep writing well-endowed, aesthetically-deprived individual, do you?).

"B-B-B-Barry."

"Ooooh! Barry! Like Barry Manilow! I'd shag 'im as well!" (loud collective oohs and aahs followed by laughter).

"Yeah, alright luv, see ya later," I interrupted getting a tad irritated by this obvious attempt at feminine intimidation of the opposite sex! [Shoe? Foot?]

"Who asked you ugly?!" was her venomous reply.

"Oh yeah? Fuckin' hark at her with a face like punched clay!" I retorted.

"Now, now, Dave," Barry intervened, "she's a human being with feelin's, you know."

"Never mind that!" she went on, grabbing Barry's belt buckle and making a gap, "let's have a look at what yev got down there!"

Chapter 10 - Meet the Ladies

The laughter was deafening as Barry pulled away, making for the door at speed. I followed him at a slower pace, trying to look unruffled and dignified, only to receive 20-30 foam squares at the back of my head followed by comments about having a small penis (which I haven't... in case you're wondering).

Outside, Barry stood waiting for me.

"SEE! Told ya what that place was like!" he said.

"Oh shut it, for fuck's sake!" My ego was feeling emotionally bruised and humiliated, so we dawdled off on our way to our destination.

I drank a cup of coffee and sucked on a tab back at the deck office, thinking about burning the sewing room down with chubby still inside. It was only on reflection that I realised that I had experienced what many women experience on a daily basis in many male dominated environments, and it gave me a different perspective when working with women in my future career. It obviously affected Barry too, as he spent the best part of an hour in the toilets fixing his hair that had been viciously ruffled up.

Another area of female dominance, on their side of the counter anyway, was the canteen. I very rarely used it due to the quality of the food (or lack of). Many of my colleagues, who were single, ate all their meals there. For Tipper, the truck driver, it was the only time he got a wholesome meal with 'greens' - that's 'peas' to you and me. Those that complained, or upset the ladies in any other way, would suffer the consequences of their actions.

Russell once informed the cook that the reason women had such small feet was so they could stand closer to the cooker. She did not appreciate this comment and it was a particularly shit old joke.

A couple of weeks later when all was forgotten, he

chomped into his breakfast which was in a polystyrene box, and found half a maggot nestled amongst his mushrooms. Not being the brightest button, I pointed out to him that perhaps he should be more worried about the other half of the maggot that was no longer in the box. He began his search with the contents of his stomach on the road outside. You would have thought that a trip to the nurse would have been appropriate, but I'm afraid that sympathy was not part of the job description for the post of factory nurse.

It was coming to Christmas and the weather was cold. This had the effect of making me hunch up against the cold and not want to do a great deal. Working on a computer you tend to be in this one position too much of the time, and one day I got up a little too quickly, causing my neck muscles to go into spasm.

"What's up wi' ye'?" asked Russell.

"My neck, I've hurt my neck!" I informed as best I could. "I got up too fast!"

"Well, that wer' a fuckin' stupid thing to do wor it?" Russell laughed and then wandered off to find someone else to talk too. Not even offering to help his fallen comrade!

I got up and made my way over to the nursing station, informing Jim on the way. It was a good distance to walk to the nursing station, being the other side of the factory, but I struggled on like a brave little soldier. On arrival, I sat in the empty waiting room next to the clinic. After a couple of minutes, a young chap walked out of the clinic, with a look of dismay on his face.

"Can you fuckin' believe it? I've nearly cut my finger off, and she's taped it together with plasters and told me to go back to work!"

I looked at the injury as he peeled back one of the

Chapter 10 - Meet the Ladies

plasters and felt queasy at the sight.

"NEXT!" came a gruff female voice from the clinic causing me to stand with a start. I walked in and was met by the blue-overalled rear end of a short, stout female of about 50 years.

"Yes. What's wrong with you?" she demanded without turning to address me.

"Err...it's my neck."

"Yes, yes, yes, what's wrong with your neck?!" she pushed impatiently.

"Umm...I think the muscles have gone into spasm." I replied sheepishly.

"Huh! Spasms, eh? And how did you do that?"

"Well...I was..." I attempted to speak.

"Never mind, let's have a look." And she placed one of her stumpy hands on my neck.

"Does that hurt?" she snapped as she tilted my head to the left side.

"No..."

"Well, there can't be anything wrong then."

"Well, try looking on the right side!" I snapped back, becoming increasingly irritated with her 'couldn't give a shit' attitude.

"Nonsense! There's nothing wrong with it! If you're not happy, you'll have to do some light duties!" she retorted with a snort.

"Look, I can't do anything 'lighter' than I already do!" I replied, exasperated.

"You lot are all the same! Like big babies!" she continued without taking breath.

"Can I..." I tried again.

"...always trying to pull a fast one. Well I don't wear this uniform because I'm stupid, you know..."

"Looked better with the spuds in it" I mumbled

under my breath.

"What was that!?" she turned to face me.

"Nothin'! Thanks, I'll be off now, thanks for your help Mother Theresa! See ya!" I moved away quickly not waiting to hear any response from Sister Sausage fingers.

"You blokes think you can pull the wool over my eyes, well you can't you know!"

Her voice faded as I stepped back into the noise of the factory. The next two weeks were spent at home with a surgical collar on my neck. Good policy, eh?

There were other areas with large amounts of female employees such as admin, sales and personnel, but I had very little contact with them. Those that I did meet were a special breed. Not all women could cope with what they had to deal with on a daily basis, but to be fair, many gave as good as they got and kept their femininity to boot, which is no mean task! Good on ye ladies!

CHAPTER 11

MOVING ON (A Little about Home)

"Keep smiling."
[Rod Reeves]

Living within spitting distance of the factory means that you have contact with employees in and out of work whether you like it or not. I lived literally five minutes from the deck area, but still managed to be late for work most of the time! The location that I lived in was a walk-through for many who parked their cars in and around the close, something that was very annoying to us residents.

Tracy and I resided in a one-bedroom purpose built shoebox on an estate built on the grounds of an orphanage which no longer exists. It was located between factories, so the smell of the place would fill the air, especially in the summer. Paint fumes were the worst, causing a lot of discomfort on the hot summer days.

In addition to this, we seemed to be getting new residents in neighbouring blocks that were housed by the Local Authority as the 'Care in the Community' [an oxymoron] policy introduced by the Thatcher government of the time. Now, I don't want you to think that I have any real problem with this idea, but you have to offer ongoing support for these people, agreed? It just seemed to me that once they have set them up, they are given a bottle of tablets and left to their own devices. This is okay as long as they are capable of looking after themselves, but when the wheel comes off, it is the unsuspecting member of the public who bears the brunt!

I began to notice one of our neighbours 'unusual

behaviour' during our last summer spent in the close. At first I saw him wandering around and he was usually drunk and, at first, was just shoeless. But after a while he was devoid of any clothes other than his three quarter length brown leather coat. Spending most of his time asleep on the grass outside his flat, he would occasionally get up and follow people around the close, mumbling inaudible comments.

One morning at about 7am, I was looking out of my front room window with a cup of tea after finishing a night-shift, when he appeared from his block, butt-naked, with a large kitchen knife in his hands. He proceeded to chase after terrified Rover workers walking through the close, which I thought was a tad strange and potentially dangerous. So after choking on my tea, I managed to dial 999 and ask for the Police.

After a very short while, three police cars with a dog van screamed into the close. The man had gone back into his house by this time, but I'm pretty sure that they knew all about him. This was due to the fact that the officers went straight to the house, dog in first, followed by half a dozen Bobbies. Two minutes later and out he came, trussed up like a chicken. He was unceremoniously thrown into the back of a meat wagon and I thought *"Thank fuck for that, he's finally gone!"* Or so I thought...

About a week later I was changing a wheel on our Mini 1000 in the parking bays at the side of our block, Tracy sitting on the floor beside me sipping tea. We didn't notice the screwball until we stood up, but there he was lying on the grass on the other side of the car, again dressed only in his coat and sipping on a bottle of cider.

"Do you want to go inside, Love?" I asked, although it was in fact a directive rather than a question. For the first (and probably the last time ever), Tracy complied without a "Don't tell me what to do" rebuke. I continued what I was doing, conscious of every move of the pissed-up mad-man lying six feet away from me.

"I don't give a damn about your woman!" His voice broke the silence and my arsehole began to expand and shrink at an unbelievable rate of knots.

Fuck! He's gonna kill me! I thought.

"I don't give a damn about your woman boy!" he repeated, but this time the volume and aggression in his voice increased. I picked up my claw hammer and held it tight, tapping at the wheel brace as I tightened the nuts on the wheel.

"What's your problem, mate?" I challenged, showing no sign of nervousness...I hoped.

"I don't give a damn about your woman and I don't give a damn about you!" He sat up and was becoming more visibly aggressive.

If he comes near me, I'm gonna put the hammer straight in his head, I thought, and stood up to look straight at him.

I made a conscious decision to use tact and diplomacy as he became even angrier. I'd seen enough TV where the nutter had been talked around by the brave negotiator. Why wouldn't it work for me? I'll talk to him calmly, pacify him and walk away without incident.

"Look mate, if you don't fuck off I'm gonna put this hammer straight in your cunt of a head okay?" I decided at the last moment to throw away the tact and diplomacy theory and use a more direct approach. Well, believe it or not, it had the desired effect, and he got up and wandered off back towards his block. At the same time, I tweaked a nervous fart.

Not that mad after all, I thought to myself.

Another of our mental unfortunates (politically correct, eh?), lived in the same block as us, but on the top floor. This individual worked at the plant somewhere which was obvious by the fact that he always had his company jacket on, and I had seen him within the confines of the factory on a few occasions. Well, I think he worked there. Anyway, he wasn't at the extreme of our previously mentioned nutcase, and 95% of the time he would be walking around as if he was in a rush to get somewhere, or nowhere to be seen. He always carried a rolled up newspaper in his hand or had it stuffed into the back pocket of his trousers.

He was a stocky fellah with grey hair and an obvious broken nose. He seemed harmless enough, but a pattern of behaviour began to appear, usually when England were playing an important match, or any match for that matter!

A large Union Jack would appear hanging from his front room window on the 2nd floor and he would hang out shouting abuse to passers-by as if he was on the terraces at a football match.

"Shut the fuck up you nutter!" I heard one chap shout at him one day from a neighbouring block on the opposite side of the road.

"OOOOOOOOOOOO, AAAAAAAAAAAAAAA, WANKAAAAAAAA!" was the hooligan's reply, coupled with a matching gesticulation directed back across the street.

Italia 90 World Cup was fast approaching and we all began to brace ourselves for the onslaught. As England bounced through each round his antics got louder and lasted longer, so when the semi-final against Germany came round we waited with baited breath to see what would occur.

The jovialities started at about 1pm on the day of the semi-final, with the flag appearing early, backed up by '101 patriotic tunes' blaring out of his stereo into the

Chapter 11 - Moving On (A Little about Home)

street.

I was working a 2pm-10pm shift on the day, so shared the misery of a penalty shootout loss with a few thousand colleagues. By all accounts it went very quiet as the nutter went out to share his grief in the pub with his mates.

I returned home feeling pretty depressed too, and got into bed. I had just drifted off to sleep when I heard the cries of a bear caught in a mantrap coming from outside the front of the block. Realising quite quickly that there had been no bears in Rednal since medieval times, I went to investigate the source of the noise.

I looked out of the front room curtains through a crack, leaving the lights off so as not to be seen. There was our local hooligan neighbour, on his knees, arms outstretched, wailing at the top of his voice! He was facing the flag hanging from his window and wailing! He then got up and began pulling up the 'FOR SALE' boards outside the block, smashing them on the ground in anger.

Tracy joined me and we watched like excited school kids as he danced up and down the road taking out his anger and frustrations on the other 'FOR SALE' signs up and down the street.

Then, without warning, he stopped, crouched down on his knees, pursed his lips and holding out an outstretched arm, the forefinger and thumb rubbing together and making a 'kissing' noise as he spoke:

"Come on, Martin, it's okay!" he called gently.

"Who the fuck is Martin?" I asked Tracy.

"Don't swear!" was her useful reply.

Out of the darkness came the local pain-in-the-arse, bin-bag-ripping, piss-smelling tom cat that was used as target practice by pretty much every other cat owner in the close who had seen their pets getting shagged or beat up by it.

"What sort of name is Martin, for a cat?" asked Tracy.

"Mad cat mad fuckin' owner. Seems fairly obvious to me, love! I replied.

"Don't swear!" she replied backed up by a dead arm.

The tom cat jumped into his 'dads' arms and they walked into the block, and thus ended the night's proceedings.

I had my suspicions about the bloke who lived upstairs from us as well. He was a quiet 30-something professional who for some reason took a real interest in our cat, Casper. Prior to his arrival, Casper was never away from the flat for more than an hour. When he arrived she would go missing for hours on end, and one day he told me that he had been playing with her in his flat. He had also been taking photos of her on the grass and sat in the trees. I wouldn't have thought anything of it, but this bloke never had female (or male, for that matter) company.

"I bet he's got her up there now in stockings and suspenders, lying on the bed taking photos of her for his cat fetish magazine," I once theorised.

"Don't be a pratt!" was Tracy's rebuff.

Fortunately, Casper had been snipped early on, so I didn't worry about any unwanted pregnancies.

Casper was loved by all the local residents, particularly cat-fetish-man, and was a welcome sight returning home after a long hard day at work. She had a fuss off everyone in the block and was as gentle as a mouse, until she met one when she would then torture and eat it! This was a complete contrast to the wild animal that first arrived on our doorstep.

I was working as a greengrocer in a shop in Coventry during the summer of 1987, not long after we had moved into the flat. Being an animal lover, I tried to convince Tracy that it would be nice to have a pet around the place.

Chapter 11 - Moving On (A Little about Home)

"I don't like cats - they scratch!" she would argue.

"But Love, you've been living with German Shepherds for most of your life, how can you be scared of cats?"

"Shane and Tara are not vicious. Cats are!" she responded.

"I can't get out of the fuckin' chair at your mom's, because Shane sticks his nose in my crotch and starts growling, and as for Tara, I haven't seen her yet! She just hides behind the sofa growling and wailing like a banshee! How can you be scared of cats!?"

"Oh, alright, alright...but it's got to be grey, okay?"

Why do women always put conditions on everything?

Working in the opticians next to my shop was a lovely middle-aged woman called Sue who told me about some farm cats who had just had kittens and who were ready to go to homes.

"Farm cats are much better than town cats." She informed me.

Saturday night came, and after work, armed with an empty banana box, I followed her into the depths of Meriden just outside Coventry, to a farmhouse in the middle of nowhere. She had hands like a boxer did the farmer's wife, and the build to match topped off with thick ginger curly hair. Behind her stood her husband, a small bespectacled man in complete contrast to the buxom woman squeezing my hand!

"They're in the garden. Have a look, Love," she indicated to the garden which was a small field with a swimming pool in the middle surrounded by chairs, barbeque and other expensive looking garden features. (Who said farmers are poor?). Next to the pool, playing as kittens do, were three of the fluffiest, cutest little balls of fur on legs you could ever hope to see. Two were bright ginger and the other one was...grey!

"George, go and put some food on the pantry floor and shut the door to keep them in." she instructed.

George carried out these instructions like an obedient dog, going into the pantry which was a large room next to the kitchen where we stood. No sooner did the bowl of meaty mush hit the floor, there were three kittens surrounding the bowl, eating greedily. His wife then took the box from me and handed it to George.

"Now, pop the grey one in there." She instructed him again.

"What? Me?" he quivered.

"Oh get on with it! Just be firm!" she barked impatiently, and with this, George walked back into the living room with a look of trepidation on his face.

"Cuppa tea?" she invited.

After a couple of minutes, George returned to the kitchen, still in possession of the box, but now he was wearing a wax coat, garden gloves and Wellington boots.

What is he doing? I thought, looking to his wife for an explanation, but she just looked at him, turned her eyes up, and carried on talking to me about the price of potatoes.

I watched as George opened the door and stepped into the pantry, closing the door behind him. Silence fell for about 10 seconds, then utter mayhem broke out as tins, buckets and other containers started to bang and crash onto the floor. A chill went down my spine as the screams of the kittens filled the air mixed with hissing and growling.

"Oh for heaven's sake!"

The wife cut off from our chat and walked into the pantry. George reappeared looking breathless and dishevelled.

"They're wild, you know, wild!" He gasped as he

Chapter 11 - Moving On (A Little about Home)

straightened his coat.

Moments later, his wife appeared with the grey kitten tightly squeezed into her ample bosom as she stroked it so firmly that I thought its eyes were about to pop out of its head! Holding it by the scruff of the neck, she placed it in the box and put the lid on.

"There you go," she said with a smile, handing me the box, "don't worry, it'll soon get used to being handled." She continued as she ushered me quickly to the front door.

Soon get used to? I thought as I paused at the door to my van, *Oh well, at least its grey!* For the entire journey home I did not hear a sound from inside the box, and shook it on a couple of occasions to make sure there was something inside! All I heard was a light scratching as the box tilted and the kitten steadied itself.

At home I walked into the kitchen placing the box on the floor as Tracy stood behind me.

"Now look, it's a bit frightened and not used to people yet, so don't expect to pick it up straight away." I warned.

"Great! So it's vicious, is it?"

"No, no, no. It's just a little nervous. It's a farm cat so it takes a little time..."

"Is it grey?" Tracy demanded.

"Yep! It's a lovely colour!"

"Well, let's have a look at it then," she said impatiently.

I lifted the lid to find the kitten crouched in the corner, ears back, claws out and growling.

"That's not grey, it's Tabby!" Tracy shouted.

"It's bleedin' grey! How grey do you want it?"

"Are you colour blind? It's a Tabby! It's not grey! T. A. B. B. Y!" at which she stormed off.

"Oh fukin' fabulous!" I exclaimed.

"Don't swear!" came a shout from the living room.

"Great. Fuckin' great" I said under my breath.

I decided to appeal to Tracy's sensitive side. I would pick up the kitten, put it in her arms and she would fall in love with it. I turned to the kitten which was still cowering in the box.

"Come on then," I whispered as I approached, but the hissing and growling got louder the nearer I got. I reached out my hand to offer it some fuss, then:

"RRRRRRRRAAAAAAAAAWWWWWWW!" (In my best cat).

"SHIT!" I shouted as the creature jumped from a sitting position to 3ft in the air, level with my face, like a cartoon Tasmanian devil, claws lashing out in my direction.

I dived back as it dashed along the work surface dislodging pots and containers as it searched for a place to hide. I fell back into the hall and slammed the door behind me.

"Well done Dave," came the sarcastic voice from the living room.

CRASH! BANG! Came the noise from the kitchen. I sat on the floor in the hall wondering why I had bothered.

It took about five days for Casper to finally stop creeping around the outside of the rooms and start to approach us. But when she finally did, she became a big part of our lives, and stayed with us for ten years until on her 10th life she had a head butting contest with a car and lost.

Living in a shoebox with another person and a cat, you start to feel a little claustrophobic, and tempers began to get increasingly frayed. I needed, we needed, to expand and move on for these reasons, and for the neighbourly reasons already mentioned. We began to annoy each other because there was no way of getting away from each other

Chapter 11 - Moving On (A Little about Home)

when we were at home. On one particular occasion I spent a day being an irritable bastard and continued this into the evening. Tracy decided to have a bath to escape me and relax.

Whenever I get bored, I amuse myself by taking the piss out of anything. I chose to annoy Tracy while she was in the bath by going in and out constantly and not giving her any peace.

So effective was I that she stood up in a rage, wiped everything off the pine shelf that I had fixed above the bath, picked up the top shelf (not nailed to the brackets – big mistake!) and proceeded to belt me around the head with it. This had the desired effect, and once I had gained full consciousness again, I decided to leave her alone. In addition to this, Tracy cut her finger on the corner of the shelf and decided to squeeze some of the blood on the wall, which neither of us would clean up out of principal. Tracy would tell everyone who noticed it that it was from when, 'he cut my finger during a row!' When I finally did succumb, I had to paint over it due to the lack of a cleaner able to shift it.

To save our sanity we moved a couple of miles up the road into a two bedroom house in a quiet cul-de-sac. Again, it was a purpose built home with walls that you couldn't hang pictures off without those special plugs. The garden was long and thin and at 45 degrees sloping downhill, but it was a garden, and we finally had upstairs and downstairs space at last!

It was mid-September in my first year at the plant when we moved, selling the flat for a healthy profit. We had money in the bank and were far more at ease. I decided that we needed an addition to our family, so with Tracey's consent I purchased a six week old German shepherd puppy from a breeder in Great Barr, Birmingham.

I'd always wanted a dog and Tracy, as mentioned before, was brought up with them. 'Shane' and 'Tara' belonged to Tracy's mum and dad - Sue and Rod. Tara was a 70lb black shepherd who had been ill-treated by a previous owner causing her to skulk around growling at anyone she didn't recognise. Shane on the other hand, was the dog world's equivalent to a 'dumb bastard'. Put the two together and they made a formidable team!

I had the opportunity to look after them both for a week one summer when Sue and Rod went on holiday. Tracy and I decided to move into their house so the dogs would have company. At the time, I had an escort car-derived van from the fruit and veg firm I was working for, so I thought I would use it to carry the dogs down to the park for a run.

Well, my initial attempt involved trying to walk the dogs to the van, but unfortunately, with two 70lb furry land sharks on the end of a rope (one trying to attack passers-by) I did not get very far! I decided to change tactics. I reversed the van up to the side of the house via a gully and open the doors onto the back gates. Both dogs would be squealing and yelping to get out of the house, and as I opened the gate they would scramble over each other, biting and snarling, and throwing themselves into the back of the van. Job done!

I drove to the park with Tara squealing in my ear all the way, covering my shoulder in dog phlegm. Shane sat quietly in the back on a flattened apple box. Occasionally I saw him slide past as I looked in my rear view mirror while going around corners.

The noise was deafening as we pulled into the park, and I would first have to make sure the coast was clear while reversing onto the playing field. I opened the back doors and stood well back. Out they came, fighting,

Chapter 11 - Moving On (A Little about Home)

snarling and biting, and I saw a lady a distance away pick up her 'Scottie' dog and put it under her arm.

I followed the dogs as they went wild on the grass. They looked over towards the lady with the Scottie dog and stopped. The little dog was barking furiously, and they decided to run towards the lady as she desperately tried to muffle his bark.

"Oh shit!" I said out loud. I could see the headlines: 'ELDERLY LADY SAVAGED BY GREENGROCER'S DOGS.'

"Shane! Tara!" I screamed in my loudest, deepest voice.

At this, they stopped, turned tail, and began charging back towards me!

'GREENGROCER SAVAGED BY OWN DOGS.' The headline now changed, but not necessarily for the better! To my amazement, they dived back into the van and I slammed the doors shut behind them and stood with my back to the doors, breathing a huge sigh of relief!

As the weeks progressed I assumed a modicum of control and even managed to get them to do a few things to order. I got so cocky in fact, that I even took a tennis ball to play 'fetch' with, confident of getting it back. I was taken down a peg or two when I pretended to throw the ball and saw Shane running off, followed by Tara. I found this very amusing. Shane went for it every time, but Tara stopped after a couple and proceeded to bite me on the arse to remind me who was in charge.

Our dog Anja (pronounced Anya) was no less psychotic as a pup, or as an adult for that matter!

"You wean her by putting her food on the floor and pretending to eat it. That way she will see you as another dog and will fight for the food," according to the breeder, so I tried it.

Down went the food and I did my best 'doggy-scoffing' impression. Anja looked at me with one floppy ear on a tilted head and an "I might be a puppy but I'm not fucking stupid" expression on her face. Nature eventually took its course and a hungry pup doesn't need a lot of encouragement.

The next hurdle was teething, and to prevent any unwanted furniture destruction we purchased every type of toy and chewy for her to relieve her discomfort on. Alas, it wasn't long before she discovered the wood at the bottom of our brand new television cabinet provided far more relief than a rubber bone.

This lead onto other things, and on one summer's day whilst I lay in bed with a 2pm start to look forward to, I decided to let Tracy open the back door so Anja could run in and out at her leisure. This would allow me the pleasure of a lie-in whilst Tracy went off to work.

I don't recall the time, but I was awoken by the sound of four little paws dashing in and out of the house at great speed. "Aaaah, bless her!" I thought, and decided to get up and start the day. I walked down the open plan stairs to the living room and...

"FFFFFFFUUUUUUCCCCCCCKKKKKKK!!!!!!"

My exclamation could probably have been heard some two or three miles away and may have been registered on the Richter scale.

Sat in the middle of the living room, surrounded by thick black compost, on cream carpet, and several large plants that had been potted just a few days before, was Anja. At first wagging her tail, then down and out the back door as she realised I was less than pleased to see her. Had I got my hands on her at that point, it is likely there would have been no more to tell about her. As it was, she deposited herself behind a large holly bush at the

Chapter 11 - Moving On (A Little about Home)

very bottom of the garden, and by the time I had coaxed her out I had calmed down considerably!

Learning from this incident, we made sure that she was not left on her own for any extended periods, but due to us both working shifts it was sometimes unavoidable. Whenever this occurred I made sure that everything that could be put out of reach was. This especially included a large collection of vinyl records that had been collected over a number of years at great expense. So special was it that I had it insured separately due to the value. However, the policy did not cover teething pups!

I arrived at work one day at 2pm, with Tracy working the same shift at the hospital. I was busy booking in parts when something began to bother me. I had forgotten to do something. What was it...?

"Fuck!" I realised that my record collection had not been moved and was at this time at the mercy of the puppy from hell!

"Jim! Jim! I've got to go home...now!"

"Christ, son! What's the matter?"

"I've got no time to explain! Can I borrow your car?"

Jim threw me his keys without question and I made for home.

All the way back I prayed that Anja had not found the collection; that she had somehow overlooked it; that somehow she had realised in her little puppy mind that chewing up a rare and expensive vinyl copy of *If you want blood* by ACDC was the wrong thing to do.

I pulled up outside and rushed in. The first thing that hit me was the lack of greeting. Usually I would be smothered with affection, but not today. I walked through the kitchen into the living room to be met by my worst nightmare. Sat in a crouched position, ears down, was Anja, on top of every single record we possessed. Everyone had been carried from the shelf beneath the stereo to the middle of the room and piled up. Worst of all, at the very top were the remnants of what was my most prized possession. It was my seven inch, white vinyl single by 'Whitesnake', which I had purchased through long and difficult negotiations from a fellow collector.

At first I was too shocked and upset to react or even speak.

"You little fucker!"

But this didn't last long, and I assisted her to her favourite part of the garden without one paw touching the floor. Whitesnake, however, were to have their revenge.

The next day I got up early to avoid any incidents and took Anja for a long walk onto Beacon Hill. As usual, she was frantically looking for a place to deposit a number two, but today she seemed unable to pass anything. Eventually she assumed the position and began to howl and cry as nature took its course. Curious as to what the problem was, I inspected the offending stool and let out a burst of laughter as I saw pieces of the white vinyl that had been consumed the day before sticking out of each of her logs.

"That'll teach ya!" I said as she cruised down a grassy slope on her arse.

Anja eventually grew out of these habits and settled down with Tracy, Casper and me. I can say that this was probably one of the calmest and most secure periods of my life. New job, new home, things were good.

CHAPTER 12

THE CLEANERS

"There is no such thing as a dishonourable trade."
[Paddy]

Not dissimilar to other big firms, the company employed a firm of cleaners to do all the shitty cleaning jobs that needed doing as cheaply as possible. "Why pay someone a decent wage to do a crap job, when you can pay a dim-wit pennies to do it?" was a quote I once heard from a management-type. Low wages usually meant some of your more unusual members of society being employed to do these unsavoury tasks. I'm not saying that all had questionable personal hygiene issues, but it just appeared to me that the nature of the job reflected in many of their habits of dress and behaviour. There were even a few that failed the company job interview!

One of the funniest stories I heard was when the government van arrived at the plant full of benefit fraud investigator-types. I would add that this wasn't something I witnessed myself. They came to catch up on the workers who were claiming benefits at the same time as working, and needless to say it was an unannounced visit. However, it didn't take long for the warnings to go out. Abandoned mops, buckets, floor polishers and various other cleaning kit was to be found here and there as those who were on the investigators' lists made for the nearest hideout.

Apparently, the storyteller went to the toilet during this time and as usual could find no toilet roll in the cubicle.

Question: How many men does it take to change the

loo roll?

Answer: Don't know – because it has never happened!

So, he went to the cleaner's cupboard and opened the door. He jumped back in terror as two pairs of eyes stared back at him out of the darkness. A twin pack of loo roll was thrust into his hands and the door was pulled shut in front of him. Unable to continue with his planned deposit due to the recent shock, he walked out of the toilets and was passed by a couple of suits carrying clipboards who obviously knew of all the hideouts!

You can imagine the logistical nightmare of providing toilets and wash facilities for such a large working group, and this was reflected by the enormity of facilities provided. There were small washrooms scattered here and there, but on the whole they were mainly huge rooms with ten or twenty cubicles and opposing urinals. Huge long metal sinks went from wall to wall with rows of taps for employees to wash their hands en masse.

I became aware of a young chap of about twenty years who started as a cleaner on a temporary basis. I think he was a student as he had the ability to hold a coherent conversation and used words of more than two syllables. This was in total contrast to the muppets he cleaned alongside. I assumed he was there earning a few quid while he was at university. One of his main duties was the maintenance and cleaning of the toilets in the New West.

Early morning was the worst first break. Smoking was accepted anywhere pretty much (Guilty!!), so the first thing that hit you was a thick blue smoke-filled atmosphere. The noise of rustling newspapers filled the cubicles (I mean that's just compulsory!) mixed with loud fart noises of differing types, followed by an occasional 'plop' or gushing splatter as excrement hit the water.

Chapter 12 - The Cleaners

Belching, spitting, retching and arse-scratching was all around, and worst of all - you had to hope that the cubicle you were going into didn't have a pebble-dashed bowl or worse still, a big brown log that just won't flush!

One of my absolute pet hates was the bloke who sat in the cubicle beside you who wanted to have a little chat while you were doing your business. Now I don't know about you but I just like to imagine that I am on my own when Mr Turtle comes a callin'. The last thing I want is the thought of someone in the next cubicle counting how many times it took me to mop up.

I recently had a boss who had the annoying habit of entering the only other dumper cubicle in our restroom within minutes of me. It began to feel like he was doing it on purpose. He would read the paper and occasionally say "Got much on today?" I wanted to say *"I'M HAVING A SHIT AT THE MOMENT DO YOU MIND!"* But of course this is not conducive with a successful career. To make things worse he was an 'ankle dropper', one of those blokes who drops trousers and underpants to the floor when they have a dump.

I would have to sit there waiting until he had finished trying to avoid looking at the gusset of his grand dad underpants. Not to mention the discomfort of having a blood loss to the legs and a freezing cold behind while I was waiting.

I digress.

Once this had been overcome you had to hope that you had enough loo roll to cover the seat with a protective 6" layer, and also wipe your arse once you had finished. Then it was time to wash your hands in the communal metal trough-like sink which was covered in pink industrial hand wash. I always tried to get to the end so that the large green phlegm blobs went the opposite way towards the plughole and you didn't end up washing your face with one thinking it was industrial soap.

Once break was over it was our twenty-year-old cleaner's job to tackle the mess. I think he lasted about a week, as I didn't see him at all after this.

As previously mentioned, some of the cleaners had hygiene issues to deal with themselves. Take "Burger King" for instance. He was about 6 feet 4 inches tall with a completely round shape weighing in at around 30 stone if he was a pound (or should I say kilo?).

In this world of not wanting to offend, I should be careful as to what description I give for BK. However, I will stick with plain language and say that he was the fattest fucker I have ever seen who was still able to move around without an aid of some variety. Imagine an apple with a grape on top. Draw a face on the grape, and this will give you some idea of what I am talking about. This bloke could peel the paint off the walls with his breath and I don't think in all the time I was there I ever saw him change his clothes. Most of the time he sat on a huge floor polisher that was forever breaking down, and may have had something to do with the weight it was carrying, perhaps?

Amazingly, 'BK' was in fact a very intelligent and articulate individual using many words of more than three syllables that was way beyond most of the people he cleaned up after. This was a shock to many as he was such a quiet individual most of the time except when he needed to address anyone who questioned his appearance.

On one occasion, a gobby dislikeable chap stood bravely amongst a group and shouted: "Have you seen the shit on the back of your neck?" to which he got a few smiles, but he laughed nervously when he realised no one had fallen over with hysteria. BK dismounted and walked

Chapter 12 - The Cleaners

his huge frame over to the clown looking down on him in a menacing fashion. I thought the clown was about to get some physical retribution when: "No! I haven't! But then, I'm not a fucking contor-tionist, am I?"

The clown looked up in terror at the monster with a brain standing before him and muttered, "I was only joking. Honest!"

"Oh, I see," was BK's calm reply, "Ha ha", and back he went to his polisher, driving away slowly and leaving the clown smiling nervously at his colleagues.

In the Old West the facilities were not as modern as the New West and it showed. There was an old fellah (name escapes me, sorry!) who was the resident shit house cleaner all the time I was at the plant. I saw him most days I ventured down the old west, with his bucket and cleaning kit in his hand. On one particular occasion I saw him cleaning the cubicles with his brush, moving onto the urinals with no gloves to protect his hands. To my disgust I saw in his non-brush hand a sandwich that he chomped on as he brushed. Not very hygienic you may say, but it was made worse by the fact that half way round the line of urinals, he changed sandwich hands!

Needless to say, the turnover of staff was very high and it meant that many new starters had to learn the ropes very quickly. Even though cleaning is a fairly straightforward operation, a little skill was required to use the equipment provided.

"I reckon it was the Mafia!" Russell threw his theory of the assassination of JFK to the group.

"Bollocks! They might be powerful criminals but they haven't got enough clout to pull it off!" I argued.

"What about the Cubans then?" Alan added, "they must have been pretty pissed off after the Bay of Pigs!"

"Did the Yanks kill all their pigs??" Russell asks

Living in a Plant

genuinely.

"Oh for fucks sake!" exalts Jim.

"I reckon it was the CIA and the Army so they could get the war in Vietnam they wanted," I continued, trying to look clever even though I had read the theory in a magazine article at the dentists.

"I reckon it was that pillow-biter without the eyebrows and his bum friend." Russell interjected, returning to the discussion.

"What?" Alan asks.

"Ye know? Them blokes in that film TJK with Kevin Costner," Russell attempts to explain.

"J F K! Ye thick cunt!" insults Jim.

"Bollocks!" Russell shows Jim the middle finger.

"Where were you when Kennedy was shot, Jim?" I ask, knowing I was about to get a good answer.

"Well, that's a story..."

"I thought it fuckin' might be!" Alan read my mind.

"De ye want to hear or no?"

"Yeah Jim, go on, ignore him!" I encourage.

"Well..." Jim settled himself, "...I'd just been made RSM and was organising a regimental dinner in a secret bunker down south...can't say where." Jim tapped the side of his nose.

"Why wor it a secret?" enquired Russ.

"So no one knew where it was!!" Jim looked at Russ, hands out and palms up, shaking his head.

"Oh," none the wiser.

"Anyhow, captain of our regiment at the time was Ted Heath..."

"Ted Fuckin' Heath, prime minister Ted Fuckin Heath?" exclaimed Alan, turning in his chair to look at Jim. "What the fuck was Ted Heath doing there?"

"Havin' his dinner!" Jim turns his look of disbelief to

Chapter 12 - The Cleaners

Alan "and he wasne' PM at that time anyhow, any other stupid questions?"

At this point, Leroy walks into the office from the deck to pour himself a cup of tea.

"Another bollocks story Jim?" he asks.

"Come on Jim, get on with it!" I push, eager to find a hole in his story.

"Okay, okay. Well, Monty was doing the after dinner speeches, once we had eaten..."

"Was Monty still in the army in 1963?" asks Alan.

"Ey, he was," Jim confirmed, "anyhow, I was doin' the Master of the Ceremony bit when..."

"Hang on," I interrupt, "wasn't Ted Heath in the Navy?"

"Fuck me! Yeah, he was!" Alan confirms. "So, what was he doin' as a Captain in your Regiment?"

"Ah. Well. Yes. I'm glad you asked." Jim's eyes darted from side to side as if he was writing and reading the story as he went along. "Because this was just before he transferred to the Navy...well..."

"Are they allowed to do that?" Russ asks.

"Do what?" Jim asks becoming increasingly irritated.

"Transfer from the Army to the Navy?" Russ clarified.

"Does it really matter...? Anyway, so this private whispers into Monty's ear, at which Monty just went white and sat back in his chair. So I rushed over and said 'What's wrong Monty?', and he says, 'It's Kennedy, Jim. They shot him!' and I..."

"So what happened to his stiff upper lip?" Alan asks as he gets up from his chair at the same time as Russ begins to laugh falsely.

"Ye dinny even know what you're laughin' at do ye, stupid!" Jim continued shaking his head and pointing at Russ. "So, I said, 'Pull ye sell together Monty' and brought the dinner to order, announcing the news..."

"What was Ted doin'?" I ask with a hint of sarcasm.

"Oh, he was cryin' his eyes out the fuckin'..."

WWWWWWRRRRRRRRRRRRRRR BANG! The noise made us all jump up with a start as the thin metal walls of the office vibrated viciously.

WWWWWWRRRRRRRRRRRRRRR BANG! Again the walls shuddered and a plastic board tile fell out of the suspended ceiling exposing the factory roof.

"What the fuck!" Alan shouts what we're all thinking.

WWWWWWRRRRRRRRRRRRRRR BANG! Another tile falls and we run out of the office to avoid injury, going round the back of the office to discover the source of the noise.

At that time, a new small parts store was being constructed behind our office, and as usual it was the job of the cleaners to polish the floor and paint lines. In this new area, surrounded by half a dozen pissed off males, namely us, stood a small, skinny and generally unwell looking individual of the male persuasion wearing cleaner's overalls. He was holding onto a floor polisher that was about the same size as him.

"And what the fuckin' hell doo yooo think ye doin', sonny?" Jim went into a serious gaffer mood.

"Sssssorry, it's a bit heavy an' I can't seem to..."

"Give the fuckin' thing here!" Jim interrupted angrily, "I used to have my own cleaning company in Scotland when I came out of the Army..."

"Fuck me! Man. You just can't help yourself, can you?" Leroy exclaimed.

"What de ye mean?" Jim looked shocked that Leroy doubted his word.

"It doesn't matter..." Leroy walked off waving a hand in Jim's direction.

Chapter 12 - The Cleaners

"Right! Let's show this fucking Vietnamese refugee how te work this machine!" Jim took hold of the handles and pulled the lever with his fingers.

"Fuckme!" off he went behind the polisher as it took off into a pile of plastic containers sending them skyward and all over the unpolished floor. The belly laughs were deafening, mine included, as Jim steadied himself and pressed again, crashing into a stack of small pallets at which point he let go and it stopped dead.

"See! See! I told ya..." feeble man piped up as if relieved that he was no longer the centre of attention.

"Oh eye!" Jim shouted, stamping angrily over to feeble man, "So what sort of fuckin' cleaner are ye then? A cleaner that can't clean?"

Feeble man backed off as Jim prodded his chest.

"About as much use as a limp cock in a room full of vaginas!"

More belly laughs.

"Why, I've left bigger men in a French letter ye skinny fucker! Now, get off my deck and don't come back until ye can de ye job!"

Feeble man scurried off like a smacked child followed by Jim who continued to scream inaudible comments at him, leaving us struggling for breath behind him. That was the last we saw of feeble man.

I do hope I haven't painted a 'mightier than thou' picture of my attitude towards those cleaners I met. I just tried to say what I saw. Ironically, many of the people employed by the company did see themselves as better somehow, and expressed these views even though they often moaned about being treated as low life by the management.

In the police career that followed, I was derided for my brief history at the plant by people who saw themselves as better somehow, even though they did the same job as me at the time. This attitude pissed me off no end! I mean, it doesn't matter what you do for a living, does it? I would argue that it takes a darn sight more motivation to get out of bed to do a shit job for £2.50 an hour, or even less in some cases for some of the cleaners at the time, than it would for twenty times more per hour in an office job. Agreed?

Some people aren't blessed with the brains of others, but shouldn't be looked down upon because of this fact. Remember the 1950's and 1960's when the government couldn't get the indigenous population to drive the buses and trains or clean the streets? So people from the Empire/Commonwealth had to be shipped in to fill the gaps. Then, when jobs were scarce, the same people shouted "[insert minority] Go Home!" because "they are taking our jobs!" Cheeky Bastards eh? It was those people who kept the country moving and took all the abuse and crap in the knowledge that they were carving out a better life for themselves, or so they hoped.

We can be critical of those who work and claim benefits, but if I were cleaning shit for pennies and had a wife and kids to support, you can bet your life I would probably think about doing it too. Anyway, my point is that the wheels have to go round, and I have a lot of respect for those guys and girls who did and do the jobs that most of us would not in our wildest dreams have entertained doing.

- End of Sermon -

CHAPTER 13

WHO'S IN CHARGE?

*"Yam can be in charge when I tell yem ye in charge.
Until then Fuck off."*

[Fred]

Being a "gaffer" in the plant could be a very rewarding position both financially and motivationally, yet at the same time one of the most thankless jobs any individual could hope to do. A lot can depend on where you work, how much power you actually have, how much power those you supervise <u>think</u> you have, and how much influence they have to counter your authority. If the gaffer knew the politics of his area and worked it well he could sit back and relax while the job got done. But! Get it wrong and they would fall a very long way and risk being sent to a dark hole where no further damage could be caused.

During the 1970's the unions ran the company and the track workers had the power to stop production at the drop of a hat. *"EVERYBODY OUT!"* was the war cry, I was told by older workers. If an early finish for the Friday was required, any excuse for a walkout could be found. Of course there was no real loss to the company as the tax payer owned it, and that bottomless pit of public money would fill the gaps between loss and breaking even. The stories I heard about the seventies and early eighties were more similar to that of the tales of a High School. The big kids would avoid work, upset the bosses and do everything to disrupt the class or production line in this case.

As the company was privatised the atmosphere began to change and those with the sense to realise it understood that the government safety net was no longer there.

Many understood that to survive in a global market the company had to be competitive and that meant working to the maximum. However, the absolute bottom line remained, if you upset the workers and there was solidarity amongst all of them, which was usually the case, as a Gaffer you were in for a rough ride. I mean, you can't sack everyone! Or can you?

With the introduction of 'Total Quality Improvement' or TQI for short, and the award of the 'Investors in People' badge, it became obvious that the company was trying desperately to change the attitude of the workforce. It became the job of the new Team Leaders, Facilitators (Foremen), Co-ordinators and Factory Manager to drive the change. You've heard the expression 'shit rolls down hill", well at the plant it rolled down, up and side-to-side, everyone ducking out of the way so it didn't stick to them. 99.9% of the time it would be an unsuspecting gaffer who didn't hear the "DUCK YE CUNT!" cry, who it stuck to. Never have I seen an example of the shop floor worker being so untouchable!

'The line must not stop!' that was it, and, if it did then the plant manager would want to know why. If someone needed to be humiliated and dealt with then Jim the mad Irish man Callaghan would make sure someone would pay!

Callaghan was the West Works number one man, and was without doubt one of the most nasty, ignorant, arrogant and venomous people I have ever had the utter misfortune of working for. He made everyone jump when he came down from his office in the sky, making a point of humiliating and verbally abusing those supervisors he didn't like in front of the workers.

Due to the managers falling under the "Staff"

Chapter 13 - Who's in Charge?

umbrella they were not in the same safety zone as the shop floor worker. A lack of union backing and the fear of losing their well-paid jobs would result in nothing being said in complaint against Callaghan. His lack of personnel management skills and poor professional conduct was apparent, and evidenced on one particular occasion when I was being interviewed for a Team Leader post.

I was summoned to the top floor for the 'interview' in the hope that I could become a factory platoon leader, with the responsibility of a small crew of blokes. I would be charged with conveying their problems [we didn't have issues in those days] to management, and vice versa the other way back to them.

My interviewers were Bryan Langford and a staff admin-type who was not known to me. Langford was not the most popular gaffer himself, but was harmless enough.

He was very distinctive in his appearance, being 6feet 6 inches tall with a 'coco the clown' hair style, and always wore trousers 6 inches too short and 2 sizes too small for him.

"So, Dave, I think it's important to point out what will be expected of you. I mean, you are effectively becoming a part of the Management Team, but at the same time remaining one of the shop floor workers." This was delivered in unison with lots of touchy feely hand gestures from Bryan.

"Yep. I understand" in unison with folded arms from me.

"As a leader, you will be expected to take the lead, of course, and you will have to be able to deal with people, showing respect so that you gain their trust and confidence" a head nod to see if I was still with the program "so you can, well, get the job done."

"Yep! Got that" My boredom was beginning to show.

"So, it is very important that as a leader you don't forget to talk to people as an equal" more hands and nods "even though they may see you as being higher up the ladder than they are."

"Yep." Nodding now and slipping into a coma...

"And in addition you have to remember not to belittle people or make them feel small or inadequate..."

SLAM!

The door of the office burst open and we all sat back with a start as Callaghan barged in with a look of anger on his face.

"Langford! You Fuckin' Wanker!" he screamed in his broad Northern Irish accent, "Why did ye no sort that part out yesterday? Are yee a fuckin' idiot or what?"

"But Jim, I, I..." Langford stuttered.

"As soon as yev finished fuckin' aboyt up here get ye fuckin' skinny arse in my office, understand!" He didn't wait for an answer, and I didn't think he was making a request as he slammed the door behind him.

We sat in silence looking at the door, so I decided to break the ice.

"So, Bryan" I nodded in his direction and opened my hands palms out, "you were saying?"

Second in command to Callaghan was an individual who I would describe as a slimy piece of shit, called Martin Hammersley [and that's all I want to say about him for now] and next in line were the co-ordinators who were the highest rank on the shop floor. Langford was one of them along with Paul Davis and Bryan Morgan who ran the other two shifts. Davis was a very mellow, 'no worries' type Brummie with a lurching walk and a nose so big that it arrived ten seconds before he did. Morgan, although similar in appearance, was completely the opposite in personality, panicking at the slightest

Chapter 13 - Who's in Charge?

problem and suffering from stress most of the time.

No doubt this was the main reason he was losing his hair which was jet black with no sign of grey whatsoever.

Poor Morgan was very self-conscious about his thinning top which he combed in every way imaginable in an attempt to disguise the fact. No one really took any notice until one day he decided to confide in someone about it. Obviously Morgan felt this was a safe shoulder to cry on. (What a naive twat!).

I learned from a very early stage that you never, ever, discussed anything with anyone about yourself that might be even the slightest bit embarrassing. In a monotonous environment, any release was taken advantage of to the full, and I have seen grown men cry due to the manner and amount of piss taking that went on over the smallest thing.

Needless to say, once the news filtered to the many ears about Morgan's little frailty, the onslaught began, and it wasn't long before a walk down the deck or to any part of the New West became a bit of a trial for him. Position was no protection. Much of his internal mail was addressed to 'Mr Bryner' with the appropriate (or inappropriate) nicknames being screamed at him as he walked by. Allegedly a pot of glue and a box of fibreglass managed to find its way onto his desk with a sign stating 'I hope it's the right colour!'

On one occasion, one of the walkie-talkie's that were used by supervisors for communication across the plant went missing. The first thing Morgan knew about it was when he stopped for a chat at the coffee machine with a colleague from the track, and his radio piped up:

"Bryan Morgan...over."

"Yeah, go ahead." He replied innocently.

"Bryan Morgan...are you there?"

"Yeah, go on." He replied, moving into a more open space and speaking a little louder this time.

"Bryan Morgan...over" repeated the voice on the radio causing Morgan to look down to make sure his battery light was not indicating 'Low'.

"Yeah Bryan Morgan here go on." He repeated, sipping from his coffee.

"Bryan Morgan. Are you receding!" came the loud bellowing comment.

Bryan's colleague coughed on his coffee as he attempted, but failed, to hide his outburst of laughter. Morgan threw his coffee in the bin and began stomping off towards his office shouting "Who is this!?" into his radio and got a crowded reply from a group of male voices shouting obscenities down the radio. After an intense investigation by the supervisors, absolutely nothing was found out.

Next in the group of supervisory-types came the Facilitators, or foremen. The old 'white-coats' as Jim Thompson still was, were now Middle Managers. You've met Frosty (from the 'Night Shift' chapter), well in addition we had Mickey Graham who was a 5 feet 4 inch Mexican-looking chap with a big bushy moustache. Due to his appearance he was given the name 'Gringo.' He had the quickest walk in the plant and would cover the full length of the factory a hundred times a day, surviving on coffee and cigarettes. Often he would be challenged across the expanse of the empty deck to a gunfight by whoever saw him, usually instigated by the shout "Hey, Gringo!" which he duly ignored.

For a short while we had a newly promoted foreman nicknamed 'Rodney' due to the way he looked and sounded like his *Only fools and Horses* TV show namesake. His big problem was that no one ever did anything he

Chapter 13 - Who's in Charge?

said or took any notice of him whatsoever. We would have regular extended tea breaks which he would do his best to end, only to be met by a tirade of abuse and an office door being slammed in his face. Poor chap only lasted a month until he began to show signs of a nervous breakdown and had to be moved to an area that needed little or no supervision.

'Lloyd' was a West Indian foreman covering the 5th Aisle store and staff who worked there. He was truly a 'geezer' and for some reason every time he walked up the deck the theme tune to 'Shaft' began to play in my head. He was in his mid-50's, slim, athletic and had that booming laid back voice that many mature West Indian males have. He would explain procedures and direct people in a slow, deliberate manner as if they were five-year-olds. [Which made a lot of sense for some of them] The overalls that he wore were always immaculate with a pressed shirt underneath open to just above nipple level revealing bright gold chains. Cuffs turned up showing gold watch with numerous gold rings on his fingers and highly polished patent leather shoes at the end of his razor sharp trousers.

Nothing seemed to trouble him. In fact he was the only gaffer never to be on the end of Callaghan's abuse, or even be bothered by him for that matter. His laugh was deep and booming but his vocabulary was as advanced as any person in authority. Very rarely did I see him become angry, but needless to say, even Lloyd occasionally had his buttons pressed. He was a formidable opponent when roused from his Caribbean-island-mellowness.

I once saw a mouthy little shit drive his fork lift truck into Lloyd's area and tell him to "Fuck off!" in front of a large group of employees. Lloyd, obviously bubbling inside, calmly walked over pointing and beckoning with his finger.

"Come wid me Wonka. I wan talk to you in my hoffice."

Cocky shit followed with a look of "So? What's he gonna do to me?" on his face.

Outside we heard Lloyd tearing the driver to bits with his verbal onslaught and at one point the driver was challenged to a penis-measuring contest to see whose was the bigger! After a while the silence fell and a few minutes later they both emerged, Lloyd with his arm on the driver's quivering shoulder.

"Now, I tink you hunderstand dat I am de management and you mus show me respeck at all times. OK?"

"Yeah." The driver nodded like a compliant, scolded puppy.

"Now, go on wit your work" he said as he gave the driver a patronising slap on the back of his crew cut head.

It's fair to say that the job of a gaffer is very well paid, especially from the Langford level and up. They also had the added bonus of a company vehicle for next to nothing on some tax avoiding type company scheme. In addition, believe it or not, we had profit sharing. "What?" I hear you say, "The Rover, Profit!" Oh yes! Apparently we did make a profit, and every single one of us got a share of it once a year. The amount you got depended on what level you were at, and it was one particular payment that caused the first and only walk out I ever experienced.

As hourly grade workers we could expect to get about £100 from the profit share with foremen getting a little more. But then it suddenly jumped up to about £1500 for Langford and co.

This was not a widely known fact, but on this occasion someone found out, and it didn't take long for the jungle drums to start thumping.

Chapter 13 - Who's in Charge?

It is at this point that I would like to introduce you to 'Frank' who was our shop steward. He was a small, insignificant chap, 5 feet tall, boyish stature with long, unkempt jet-black curly hair that covered half of his face. He had a bit of a stammer which may have brought about his usual shy demeanour. Frank was one of those people you see walking around holding a large square carrier bag by the handle so the retailers name can be seen in all its glory. He wore clothes his mother had bought him in the early 70's, consisting of big flared trousers and clog shoes. But don't let this description deceive you, because he was a demon inside with balls like a horny bullock. He is the only person alive who ate my wife's rice pudding and enjoyed it! A whole casserole dish full! When roused from his boyish demeanour, he became a scary man!

One thing which got his back up more than anything were gaffers of any type, and he would make it blatantly obvious if challenged by one. Rodney, during his short time with us, attempted to get Frank to do a job that wasn't in his remit. Obviously unaware of Frank's flipside and seeing this quiet little man as an easy target, he approached with a swagger and an obvious false sense of security.

Frank nibbled his sandwich, drank his tea and read his copy of the 'TIMES', which was almost as tall as he was. He ignored Rodney at first who then became very assertive in response to this rebuke.

"Frank, I'd like it done now, please!"

Frank looked up from his paper momentarily. I could see the whites of his eyes, and his top lip curling upwards showing his teeth that were covered in marmite from his sandwich. Through the locks of his black hair he had a very sinister appearance, and he responded in a hissing voice, "F-F-F-F-F-F-Fuck O-O-O-O-Of Y-Y-Y-Y-YOU !"

Rodney backed off with a look of terror on his face, and Frank carried on eating, sipping and reading as if nothing had happened.

Right, back to the plot. (WHAT PLOT?). So, as the drums beat people on the shop floor became increasingly incensed about the difference in profit share payments. A meeting was called during the first break for the shop stewards and the logistics staff, with other similar meetings taking place around the track.

"So, how come roight, that Langford gets more than me, when all he does is walk up and down the deck while I do the work?"

Sugar looked quizzically in Tipper's direction, who had decided to ask the opening question of the meeting "Because he's a fuckin' gaffer that's why moron!" Sugar answered.

"Sugar" was called so due to the fact he was a light skinned thirty something West Indian fellah who had the vaguest resemblance to 'Ray Leonard' or any other boxer called 'Sugar Ray'. He was the newest member of our crew coming from somewhere else in the plant. [How do I know where?]

Sugar probably deserved the nickname as I found out one afternoon when I decided to place my ghetto blaster on a steak and kidney pie that he had brought in for lunch. We of course exchanged unplesantries, and postured aggressively facing each other. Usually these incidents were de-escalated fairly quickly by other workers, but this time we came to blows. When I say that we came to blows, what I actually mean is that Sugar swiftly belted me 5 times before I could get him pinned down and in a position to hit him back. He may have been twice my age but he hadn't lost 'it.' Lots of shouting and pushing and pulling followed, but it all ended no sooner than it had

Chapter 13 - Who's in Charge?

started. "Just because the fellah is old/err, don't assume he aunt gonna kick the shit out of ya" was the advise I was given. Lesson learned, and mutual respect earned.

"Ah, yeah, but he's only got to stand around 'en 'e! An I've got to load the train and unload it!"

Tipper's stupidity was unrelenting as he flicked his fringe out of his eyes.

"Tipper, it doesn't matter how much work he does, he is a gaffer, so he gets more money! We're arguing about the fact that the difference is so big" I tried to explain to Tipper the reason for annoyance.

"L-L-Look. What are we G-G-Gonna do? C-C-Cos I've got T-T-To G-G-Go back T-T-T-To the lads on the T-T-T-Track with a D-D-D-D-D...Answer." Frank attempted to push the large gathering to a decision. It was Friday morning and it was obvious that an early start at the pub was the main target for most if not all of those present.

"Well, I think we aughta 'ave a show of solidarity and walk out!" a driver shouted from the back of the rest room, which was met with a ripple of agreement from the others present.

"Oi think we aughta ask for more money!" Tipper shouted over him to be met with a wall of silence.

"We're not gonna get more money Tipper, don't you see?" Sugar said with a hint of impatience.

"So, how come, roight, Langford gets more money than me when all he does..."

Moans all round as Tipper goes on.

"Shit my tit's off Tipper!" interrupts Sugar. "Can't you just not say anything, just shut the fuck up there's a good Mong."

"There ain't no fuckin' need for that!" Tipper looked hurt, or was it just vacant?

"I'll try to be nicer to you, if you try to be cleverer,

OK?"

"L-L-L-Look, A SH-SH-show of 'ands then" Frank called order and it was agreed to walk out if the rest of the people on the track agreed.

Break time had ended some ten minutes prior to this, and by this point Martin 'slimy fucker' Hammersley [Remember I mentioned him] appeared at the door with a smarmy self important look on his face.

"This is an unofficial meeting and as Jim Callaghan's number two..."

"Yeah, ain't that a fuckin' fact!" piped up an unidentified voice before he could finish.

"...eh? eh!" Hammersley looked around the room for the face behind the voice "I would like you all to return to work immediately or you will find yourselves in trouble!" he finished with a wagging finger not pointing at anyone in particular.

"P-P-P-Piss off! This is A-A-A-An official M-M-M-M-M-M-Meeting!" Frank began to heat up as the enemy intruded in his domain.

"Now, there is no need to be rude!" Smarmy continued "I'm just pointing out the facts!"

"I-I-I'm not being R-R-Rude, J-J-Just F-F-Fuckoff, this is a P-P-P-Private M-M-M-Gathering!"

I could see Frank's demonic look begin to manifest itself again, as his eyes dropped under his fringe and his teeth began to show.

"Right!" Hammersley attempted to be a little more assertive, "if you don't go back to work you will be in real danger of losing your jobs!" he said with conviction but with no weight behind it.

Someone finally snapped and shouted, "If you don't fuck off you'll lose your bastard teeth." Hammersley was now backing out the door with a white face like the slimy piece of shit he was (I really didn't like him...can you tell?)

At this, the room erupted into laughter and jeering as abuse, teabags, half-finished pot noodles and the contents of the bin followed him down the metal steps from the rest room.

A larger meeting followed only ten minutes later attended by pretty much everyone from the shop floor. We were warned that if we refused to go back to work it would jeopardise our jobs (this coming from Management through the shop stewards). Such was the concern about the threats made and the warnings from the Management, that a unanimous decision was reached:

'EVERYBODY OUT!'

And so the entire workforce had the rest of the day off pumping thousands of pounds into the local economy or 'licenced premises' as it was better known. As a direct result of this action we all received a written warning with our pay stubs telling us in no uncertain terms that we would be dealt with severely if this happened again. Someone made a lovely mosaic on the locker room wall with most of them spelling out something like 'SUCK MY CLOCK CALLAGHAN.' I'm not quite sure what the culprit was trying to say, are you?

I'm not someone who agrees with this sort of industrial action lightly, but I was in total agreement with that grievance and was happy to say that I voted to walk out. I believe that it is every person's right to show their displeasure about something in an active but inoffensive way, upheld by the democratic right to voice an opinion. Besides, there was a good film on the TV I didn't want to miss!

One occasion when everyone loved a gaffer was during the regular auditing of the company. It was in your best interests to get your nose very close to the gaffers rusty sheriff's badge as there was money to be had in large quantities. Every gaffer under the sun was on duty, and hundreds of shop floor lads hung around waiting to be directed to do something by someone, anyone! I have known groups of employees stand around for three or four hours drinking coffee, smoking and chatting while Team Leaders ran around like headless chickens counting parts. I can't really criticise due to one particular audit that boosted the family coffers quite nicely.

The audit was in full swing and as usual no one knew who was supposed to be doing what. I decided to disappear about mid-afternoon to the Old West due to the fact that there was less to count in that area and gaffers were in short supply.

I ended up in the fork lift repairers shed, the staff gone home by this time, and sat down in a well-padded chair, feet up, watching a 35inch antique television next to a very warm fire. The inevitable happened and sleep overcame me...

"...and that's the news from ITN tonight. Goodnight!" The music from the TV woke me and I stretched out like a contented cat after the best sleep ever.

Oh, that's a shame! I wanted to watch the six o'clock news, I thought, and looked at my watch to confirm the time at 6:30pm.

"OH SHIT!!" I shouted out loud to no one in particular, realising that it was in fact the news at TEN! I jumped up and headed back to the deck.

On arrival I saw that people were filtering home but the place was still busy.

"And where the fuck have you been cunty bollocks?" Jim Thompson's voice made me jump 6 inches into the air due to the stressed state I was already in. I knew I could

Chapter 13 - Who's in Charge?

get away with a lot of skiving but surely not this time, not when I was earning double time?

"Mad cunt down the Old West, Jim..." I mumbled through, "...made me count a pallet with a trillion parts in" I lied. "Bin there all fuckin' night!"

"Oh." He looked at me with suspicion. "That's alright then, as long as you weren't skiving!"

"Me Jim?" I tried to look shocked at the thought. "NOOO!"

CHAPTER 14

SHIFTING APART

"Havin' a laff."
[Andy]

"Oh man! You could get a family of four up there! I'd shag 'er!"

"And 'er."

"Fuckin' Hell! She's gotta box like a kitten's 'ead!"

"Look at that! How did he get it up there, from there?"

"That can't be right! It looks like a fresh axe wound!"

"That's very uncouth, you sick cunt!"

"Ooooh! Hark at Sasha Distel over ere!"

"eh?"

"Ma wife used te be a model ye know?"

"Fuckin' Hell Jim, it must have been a terrible accident?"

"What ye talkin' about?"

"Well don't tell me she's got that fuckin' ugly, naturally?"

"Ye cheeky bastard. C'mere…" Jim chased Alan out of the office as Sugar, Russell and I peered at the pages of a Dutch porn magazine left for us by one of the drivers as a thank you for efficient service.

"She looks like someone set fire to her face and put it out with a mallet!" Sugar informed us.

"Who does?"

"Jim's wife. Right Pig!" he added.

"I heard that!" Jim re-entered the room. "She's no' that bad!"

"She fuckin' is!" Alan backs up, getting his head shoved under Jim's armpit and his forehead warmed up with a fist.

"How did you get on with your new girlfriend, Russ?" enquired Sugar.

"Eh man! Fucking great! First night out and I got a shag!"

"Oh ar? And what's she like?" I look up from the magazine to pursue this new line of conversation with its obvious opportunity for malicious piss-take.

"She's thirty-nine, but she day look it..." he added quickly, "...and she's got a coupla kids, so she aye lookin' for an 'usband."

Russ was twenty-one, so his hormones were set on overdrive the same as anyone that age. He was from the rough end of Quarry Bank in the Black Country and still lived with his grandmother even though he was in his early twenties. Not the brightest button, he was quickly hooked by an older woman in a night club who saw the opportunity to assist him dispose of his weekly pay packet. By the time he took the cash on Thursday he was planning for the Thursday night out, and by the time Friday morning came he was already 50% lighter in the wallet.

By Monday morning he was potless and was on the scrounge for cigarettes and cash subs until the next pay packet.

"Does she take it up the arse?" Jim asked, having now released his prisoner in order to join the interrogation.

"Betta than that, we did some French kissin'!"

We looked at each other, intrigued. I mean, we all know our interpretation of a French kiss, but Russell's; was something different as we soon found out.

"Go on!" I pushed, eager to begin the sarcasm express.

Chapter 14 - Shifting Apart

"Are ya thick or what?" Russell huffs, and then settles into storyteller mode in order to enlighten his listeners.

"First, she sucks ye cock, and ye come in 'er mouth."

"Yeess..." I look at him with a frown and immediately realise that my initial suspicions were correct.

"Then, she spits it into your mouth..."

At this point Jim sat back with a look of utter disgust on his face and Sugar frowned and raised an eyebrow.

"....and you spit half back in her mouth and swallow together!" Russell finished with a look of 'isn't it obvious?' on his face.

Needless to say, we all lurched back in disgust!

"You fukin' dirty cunt!" shouts Sugar.

"That's no French kiss ye stupid yam yam twat!" shouted Jim. "If that's the way ye fukin' reproduce up there its nay wonder ye all so deformed."

"No wonder your breath smells this morning!" added Sugar with a grin.

"For fucks sake Russ!" I shake my head in disbelief as Russell puts his hands palms up in a 'what's the problem' gesture.

"Yell be pleased to know that ye may no have te worry about sharin' a cup wi that wee dirty fucker soon." Jim pointed towards Russ.

"Why's that? Jim." I enquire, having captured my and everyone else's attention.

"They're upping the build on the two hundred models so they want us on three shifts to match the track."

"Oh Great! Nights then!" Alan looked disappointed, bearing in mind he had come to his current job in order to avoid nights!

"Yell all be put in a hat with a few extras and split into three teams" Jim advised. "Oh yeah, and everyone gets te drive a forklift, so yell all be off te training school when the time comes."

And so it was that our happy little crew was pulled apart and, within a month, we began the new shifts.

In came a new fellah called 'Andy', 6ft chubby bloke from the 'nice' end of Quarry Bank. He had a real problem with Brummies who he saw as a lower form of human existence. Les came from the night shift and was a welcome addition. Sugar stayed, as did Russell, and we kept the same drivers other than Richard who was a 20-something mixed heritage fellah with a 10foot x 10foot chip on his shoulder. Alan joined his best friend, Neal, on the opposite shift so was pleased to be able to share a lift to work. The night shift stayed the same, minus Les of course, but now working days and afternoons. The gaffers swapped and changed between shifts to avoid any familiarity, so I didn't get to miss all those wonderful Jim Thompson adventures.

A late comer to Alan's shift was a young nineteen-year-old chap by the name of Adam who is best described as a 'dirtyfucking bastard' in the truest sense of the term. He was tall, skinny, with short black hair and a 'Barbara Streisand' nose on a peanut size head. Alan once saw him with his hand down the front of his trousers scratching his nuts while sitting at the table in the office. With the very same hand he started scratching his head with large chunks of something falling onto the table in front of him, with the remaining bits being removed from behind his black nails by his teeth. Then, without any thought, he began to eat his sandwiches. This was all too much for Alan who proceeded to point out what a "dirty fucking bastard" he was and banned him from touching any tea-making kit or office kit until he cut his hands off and grew a new, clean pair.

When I first met Adam it is fair to say that he had

Chapter 14 - Shifting Apart

quite a stressful life for someone so young. He was a young lad with a new baby and demanding girlfriend who would spend all his money and screw all his friends while he was at work. Not being too clever, Adam let this go on for quite a while until he saw the light and left for any other colour pasture he could find. From this point on he became a different person. Happier by far, and even cleaner on occasions due to his attempts to attract the opposite sex which on one occasion at least was rather successful.

During a shift handover Alan told us, on the quiet, about Adam's new girlfriend. He advised us that Adam had brought a photo booth picture of them both into work for the blokes to see. Andy decided to approach Adam so we could get a look at the photo. He waited as the office filled with the two shifts during change over and saw Adam appear from the deck in a chirpy whistley type mood.

"Alright, Ad? How's tricks?" asked Andy.

"Fuck off you fat cunt!" was Adams response. (Did I mention that they hated each other?)

"Eh, eh, eh! There's no need for that! I was just trying to be sociable. I mean, if we're going to share an office we may as well get on!" Andy tried the diplomatic approach.

"Yeah, alright. I'm sorry." Adam obviously wasn't but the venom had left his voice.

"So, you're courting again then, Ad? Where's she from?" Andy already knew of course.

"Halesowen."

"Oh yeah? What's her name? I might know her. I'm from round there."

"Sarah." Adam's guard was down and the walls had been breached. "I've got a photo here in my wallet, have a look," he said as he produced his wallet and pulled out the 2" x 2" photo.

At this point, I was sitting on the edge of the table next to Andy, eagerly awaiting a view and purposefully not showing any interest. I had also purposely positioned myself with my back to Adam, facing Andy. I took hold of the photo from Adam and looked with stealth so Adam was focused on Andy's reaction. She was Adam's twin! In fact the only difference was the long curly hair on her head! So alike were they that if Adam had not been in the picture I would have accused him of blagging us by having his photo taken wearing a wig just so he could pretend he had a girlfriend! She was a fucking pig!

It was one of those moments when you want to burst into fits of laughter, but couldn't even show a hint of humour because it wouldn't be fair to the lad. I walked to the door, trying not to rush, with Alan looking at me with a knowing grin. Unfortunately for Andy, he could not hide his expressions due to being sat directly in front of Adam who was eagerly awaiting his opinion on the new love of his life. I stood at the doorway so I had a quick escape route should my convulsion overcome me. But I desperately wanted to see Andy's reaction.

Andy looked down to the photo and then up at Adam, then down at the photo again. His face began to flush red and his lips tightened together.

"Well?" asked Adam, "What ya think?"

Back up at Adam, back down to the photo, face now beginning to purple up, eyes welling and cheeks pulled in as he bit on them. He handed the photo back to Adam and stood up. Not daring to open his mouth, he gave the double thumbs up sign and a wink and walked as casually as he could out of the office.

"Somethin' wrong with 'im?" asked Adam.

Andy walked out and I followed him out of the fire

Chapter 14 - Shifting Apart

door onto the road outside.

Shit did we Laugh!

We began to calm down again as Russell appeared walking up the road on to the deck after clocking in.

"What's up wi' yow pair of cunts?"

He said hello in his usual manner, and I explained what had happened, Russ decided to have a look too not wanting to be left out of the most exciting event in the day.

"Be nice now Russ," I said, "after all, she is his girlfriend!"

"Yeah, yeah," he replied, "I ay a complete bastard ya know!"

We followed him into the office to finish our tea and watch the show, knowing full well Russ would be less than subtle and would take the heat from all of us.

"Gis' a look then, Ad." Russ wasted no time.

"At what?"

"At the photo of ya new ride!"

Adam produced the photo, looking chuffed that so many men desired to look upon the beauty of his new girl.

"Fuck me!" Russ exclaimed as he looked at the picture, "Are ya kiddin' Ad? If I was in a bedroom wiv 'er and she wor naked, I wouldn't know which end to stick me cock in!"

"What ye sayin'?" Adam looked confused.

"I'm sayin' my missus' cunt is betta looking than that fuckin' pigs face!"

Fortunately, with the two shifts present we were able to separate Adam and Russell as they exchanged windmill-like blows, but it was a while before Adam would speak to Russ again.

Strangely enough, well perhaps not, Adam's Dad

had many of the same traits as his son, except in genetic appearance. Questions had been asked about the complete dissimilarity between them, but his dad, Reg, denied any rumours of adoption or coalman involvement. Perhaps it was more likely to be the bin man? He had one of those clipboard and roam type jobs that people had here and there.

He was a filthy, bigoted racist who was the factory scrounger, forever helping himself to tea and coffee from different offices, including ours, until one day Neal (Alan's mate) politely told him:

"If you want to keep drinking it, then donate to the tea fund!"

I would suggest that had you been the recipient of such a request then you would have understood a donation to be cash. Yes? Well, half an hour later Reg returned with a smug look on his face.

"'E are then!" he said in a cocky manner.

"What?" Neal looked at Reg confused.

"Ye wanted me to give me share, so 'ere it is!"

Reg held out about fifteen teabags of differing shapes and a half jar of some unknown brand instant chicory and coffee. The teabags had that off-white look about them as if they had been in a moist area that dried out in the hot weather, like an overall pocket.

"You fuckin' dirty tight-arse bastard!" Neal remarked.

"Eh??"

"You could peel a fuckin' orange in your pocket couldn't ya!"

"What ya talkin' about?" Reg looked shocked.

"Where did ya find that? In the restrooms, leftovers I suppose, ye dirty fucker!"

"No!! I got them out me locker!"

"Oh yeah? And how long they been in your locker,

Chapter 14 - Shifting Apart

Reg?"

"Umm, I don't know. They were in there when I got it coupla years back.

"Well. What I suggest you do…" Neal put his arm around Reg's shoulder and calmly walked him to the door, speaking in a low, calm voice, "…is take your snotty teabags and 10pence a jar coffee, shove them up your arse and fuck off somewhere else for your hot drinks. OK dirty bastard?"

"I will, I will. I can get a drink anywhere in this place. They all know me." Reg tried to look defiant.

"Yeah, I can imagine you're very popular, so go on then, fuck off!"

Neal waved Reg off signalling the end of Reg's free drink era on the road receiving deck.

The shift change had come about as the first Gulf War against Iraq had begun, and we had pretty much 24-hour news coverage as the Allies prepared for war. There was lots of posturing and gesturing by many of the younger male workers, Russ being the most vocal.

"I'd goo if it kicked off big time!" he would shout regularly. The obvious potential of two million Iraqis joined by Muslim sympathisers across the region made the possibility of conscription very real. A radio broadcast overheard by Russ suggested that 19-25 year olds could be getting papers at any time if the situation escalated. So when the bombs began to drop and the reality began to dawn, Russ began talking about marrying his 'French-Kissing' girlfriend.

In a very non-politically-correct environment, people spoke their mind, and an element of friction between Muslim and non-Muslim workers began to manifest. It was passed down from high that we should be sensitive and not upset people from the Muslim community within the plant, and try not to be too patriotic about the war etc etc. The day after 'The Sun' newspaper printed the 'SUPPORT OUR BOYS' front page with the squaddies face emblazoned on the Union Jack. Needless to say, sensitivity went by the by and areas of the factory looked like they were holding Royal Jubilee parties all over again.

"It's fuckin' racism, man!"

"That's bollocks Richard! It's called patriotism!" I tried to point out the difference as I saw it to our new truck driver with the big chip.

"That's the same thing, the same fucking ting! Patriotism, racism, it's the same fucking ting!"

"Listen. If I decide to support our troops who are going to liberate a country and help stabilise the region and prevent a mad bastard with a big bushy moustache from becoming the King of Greater Iraq, and I do this by flying the Union Jack, does that make me a racist?!" I found it difficult to not get angry as I knew this was the reaction Richard was after.

"I might find it offensive." He replied.

"Are you saying that you find the flag of your country, offensive??"

"No man," he replied hypothetically, "I said I might, and so might others."

I continued, "We live in one of the most free and liberal countries in the world. I wonder what would happen if I went to India or Pakistan and told them to take down their flag because I found it offensive? They would probably hang me by the balls with it, and fuckin' rightly so!" I was getting a little bit extreme but was determined to make my point.

"Dat is different!" Richard threw his arms up as if to show contempt for my point of view.

"Its exactly the fuckin' same you annoying cunt!" I

Chapter 14 - Shifting Apart

finally cracked.

"Its racism! This country is run by them, and so is this fuckin' factory!" a stabbing finger pointed in my direction caused me to stand up from my chair. I had every intention of punching Richard in the face when,

"What do you know about racism Buay?" Les spoke for the first time during the heated conversation in a quiet, questioning voice directed at Richard.

"What do you mean, man. I'm black! I know about it!"

"What colour is your Mama?" Les probed.

"She's white," he said quietly, "and my dad is from the Homeland - Jamaica." He added loudly and with more pride.

"So, you're as white as you are black then?" Les added.

"Yeah man, whats your fuckin point." Richard became sheepish as his multi-cultural background was opened to the conversation.

"When I came over to dis country in de fifties, we were treated like dirt by the locals. Spat at, beat up. Nigger! Sambo! Wog! We were called. 'No Blacks' on the signs we saw. But we made a life for ourselves and I have seen this country change for the better."

"What your point, Daddy?" Richard interrupts without manners.

"Don't call me daddy, I'm not your daddy, and don't talk to me about racism, you wouldn't know what it was if it kick' you in de face. You are just a hangry little buay wit' de wrong hattitude." Les finished.

"Man, if you weren't so old..." Richard started to say but was interrupted by Les.

"What? What would you do?" Les stood up with his stocky frame and huge workman shovel like hands clenched. He had anger in his eyes and they were looking straight at the disrespectful Richard.

"You tink you can whip dis old man! Well!? Come on! Try me for size!" Les closed the distance between them but Richard backed off, real fear in his eyes, turning whilst waving back and shouting:

"You just don't understand!"

"I do hunderstand, you are just hupset because you are not a proper black man like me!" Les shouted after him, visibly calmer as he flicked his hand from the wrist and sucked his teeth after Richard.

"Don't tink dat all black people are like him, Daved. He is just bitter and hangry about everything..." Les sat back down picking up and sipping his tea then continuing, "...I see racism from all sorts of people to all sorts of people, not just white against black. Man, if he lived in some places he would have someting to shout about, and would be shot or hung for shouting about it!" He had a little laugh to himself for some reason, and then went on, "Dis country is not perfect and racism is all around, but we can fight it and kick it into touch. But man, he jus' gets everyone all riled up and hangry! Do you want another cup of tea?"

I was to have many more heated discussions over similar matters with Richard, but strangely enough he never brought the subject up again in front of Les.

At the rear of our office a new 'small parts' store had been built. Racks of plastic boxes filled with bits of metal used to fix bigger bits of metal together...look, I just worked there, and I don't know what they were for! I was informed that Martin 'The Wanker' Hammersley [Remember him?] had been sent to Japan on a 'fact-finding mission' or 'free holiday' as it should be known, saw how it worked and put the concept into place at the

Chapter 14 - Shifting Apart

factory. For this he apparently received £5000 and a new car from the 'Bright Ideas' fund. (Takes the piss!).

Working in the store were 'Phil', 'Mac' and 'Big Ears' who got this nickname because, well, he had fucking enormous ears. Obviously we were very sensitive about his feelings in this matter. Phil was just Phil, [Sorry it's hard to describe the indescribable] but Mac was a total 'geezer' who became a solid friend as we got to know each other. Many couldn't stand him because of his brash nature and 'I love me' attitude, but I see it from the perspective that there is a thin line between confidence and arrogance. Usually those who don't have much confidence call it arrogance. Anyway, I enjoyed his company from day one so the rest can just fuck off.

When Mac looked in the mirror he didn't see the 5ft 11inch stocky-but-slightly-flabby individual with froggy eyes and a bullfrog neck. He saw Mel Gibson's young head on Arnie's body and he loved it! Strangely enough so did many of his lady friends. Those that didn't succumb to his charm and tried to take him down a peg or two usually ended up on the wrong end of his quick wit.

He once told me that he approached a girl asking her; "Haven't I seen you somewhere before?"

To which she replied; "Yeah, that's why I don't go there anymore." Turning to her friends in a smug 'fuck off' way. (His description).

Mac replied "Oh, Really? I thought it was because everyone thought you were a pig faced fuckin' arsehole!"

Possibly not the kindest thing to say, but hey, she started it!

We did socialise on many occasions and I once went with him to his local gym for a spot of weight lifting one sunny day. As usual, in these types of places it was full of large men and a couple of women posing for each other in the wall mirrors, and I felt a little out of place. I was not ashamed of my physique though, and was in fairly good shape and relatively fit, so I began to get stuck in and warmed up for 10 or 15 minutes. During this time I saw Mac pick up a few weights, make a few growling noises and put them back down. Not really getting a sweat on, just checking his technique in the mirror.

"Ready to go, Dave?" Mac shouted walking towards the changing rooms, not giving me any choice in the matter. Within 10 minutes we were in the pub where Mac proceeded to down six pints of lager followed by a Chinese takeaway and a four pack! Top Bloke and that's why I loved him!

Amongst the new drivers we had Gaz Lee who was of a similar ilk to Tipper, only a bit thicker if that was at all possible. He was short, stocky, in his late 30's and lived in the hotel "yumca" as he called it or "Y.M.C.A" to the rest of us.

He lived there for most of his adult life as he spent most of his money on beer and fags. He was a regular target of piss take because he didn't have a clue you were taking the piss which on many occasions just took the fun out of it.

During quiet evenings in the summer the crew would play cricket or football on the road outside the deck, and if we didn't have a ball or bat we would entertain ourselves by hanging off the roller shutter doors and seeing who could go the highest before your bottle went. Gaz joined in one day after we decided to give him a bit of encouragement.

"Guon Gaz! You can do it man!" I said and pushed Gaz towards the roller shutter door.

"No way, Man. I don't like heights!" he replied shaking his head.

Chapter 14 - Shifting Apart

"Russ has gone the highest so far. You're not gonna let that fuckin' yam yam beat ya, are ya?" Sugar pushed the issue.

"Yeah, Gaz! Done by a fuckin' Yam Yam?" I added, seeing Gaz tense up.

He twisted his shoulders and neck like a boxer about to fight and I knew the thought of being outdone by Russ, who was fond of calling him a 'thick Brummie twat' amongst other things, would be the last straw.

"Roight! Fuck it! Fuckin' Yam yam my arse!" he responded with a look of Rocky Balboa type defiance as he strode towards the roller door.

The bottom pole was at waist height waiting for the next contender, and Gaz took hold looking over his shoulder at Russ. "Send it up then!" he shouted with a look of defiance on his face.

Russ smiled a demonic smile and pressed the 'UP' button on the control pad.

The doors when operating would rise to about 15 feet, which was the maximum anyone had gone bearing in mind this was leg-breaking territory. After this point the bottom pole would begin to roll in the canvas and was an area no one would be stupid enough to go too - except Gaz!

"Go on Gaz! Do it man!" Andy encouraged.

"Man's a lunatic!" Les shook his head.

The door got higher. 9ft. 10ft. 11ft.

"Yev done 'im Gaz ya mad cunt!" Andy shouted.

12ft. 13ft. 14ft.

"Gaz! Drop man! Let go!" Sugar shouted with a hint of concern in his voice.

I began to get concerned as the distance to the pole rolling the canvas in was getter shorter and Gaz's feet were rising even higher from the floor.

"Gaz! Gaz! Let Go!" I shouted.

"No man! I'm goin' all the way! All the fuckin' way!"

"Oh shit!" The thought was shared by all as we looked at each other momentarily then back towards Gaz.

"Switch it off Russ!" someone shouted, but Russ had the devil in his eye.

Then Gaz's arms disappeared into the canvas up to his elbows.

"AAAARRRGH!!!" Gaz shouted out loudly as the roller came to a halt when Russ finally pushed the 'STOP' button.

"Ye comin' down ya thick Brummie twat?" Russ shouted.

"Yeah man, get me down." Was the reply from an obviously in pain Gaz.

Russ pressed the down switch and with a jolt the pole unrolled. Unfortunately, Gaz's grip had been broken and he arrived on the floor well before the roller door. We all stood in silence as Gaz rolled on the floor clutching his ankles, moaning pathetically.

Russ insisted on going to the nurse's station with Gaz 'to make sure he was alright', but I think he was enjoying Gaz's discomfort, and Gaz was in too much pain to complain. We didn't see him again until about eight weeks later and he wasn't on his usual truck, he was carrying a clipboard with him.

"How ya doin' kidda?" I asked with genuine interest as he came into the office.

"Great ta Dave, no thanks to that tosser!" Gaz indicated to Russ.

"Eh, eh, calm down. Don't become belligerent," Russ replied.

"Why aren't ya on the trucks any more cocker?" I deflected his attention back to me.

Chapter 14 - Shifting Apart

"Well, last week I came back for a medical, ye know, te see if I was fit for work..."

"Oh yeah..." I nodded

"...and the nurse like, sez, how much exercise do ya do and shit like that, yeah?" he continues as I nod, "... Well she sez 'how much do ya drink?' and I sez 'about 15 pints'. Then she sez, 'well that's a lot to drink in a week', and I sez, 'no love, that's in a day'. Well! She hit the fuckin' ceiling and took me licence off me until I cut down. I've got te see my doctor every week so I can prove it too. Bit 'arsh eh?"

"Yeah!" I nodded, trying to look surprised.

"'Ere e is! The thick fuckin' flyin' Brummie cunt!" Andy broke the calm with his big mouth.

"Bollocks fat cunt!" Gaz retorted.

"I can lose weight mate - you'll always be a fuckin'mong!" Andy replied sarcastically.

"If you're so clever, why does it take you all day to do 'The Sun' crossword, Andy?" I had decided to shatter Andy's illusion of higher intelligence to everyone.

"Fuckin' Brummies, stickin' together, eh Russ?" Andy sits down, lighting a fag.

"In fact, what was the answer you gave to a five-letter word – spontaneous reaction to a comical event?"

"I can't remember." Andy lied.

"How was it you spelt it?" I paused, pretending to try to remember..."Oh yes. Answer being laugh, which you spelt L-A-F-F!"

"Ha ha." Andy began to squirm as Gaz smiled, enjoying the moment.

I went on "Only four letters, so he adds an 'E' on the end!"

"Yeah man! Everyone knows there is only one 'F' in Laff!" (Gaz didn't help).

"Isn't that what we use on the roofs of houses?" Russell looked serious.

"Want a cup of tea, Gaz?" I gave up having made my point.

"Y'all reet Gaz?" Jim entered the office immediately putting his face close to Gaz's in a Sgt Major fashion. "Fell off ye truck, my arse!"

"I did! I did!" Gaz looked panicky as if he'd been found out, not realising Jim couldn't give a shit either way.

"Ye fuckin' liar! Ye were hangin' off the roller doors weren't ye! Tey fuckin' stoopid te know when tea let go!" Jim pretended to be the angry gaffer "Ye cannie hide it from me sunny, people talk te me!"

"Prove it ye fuckin' sweaty sock!" Gaz jumped up and walked with a hobble as quickly as he could out of the door, not wishing to be interrogated further.

Jim smiled, happy with his successful wind up session with Gaz. "He should have landed properly, then he wouldne of hurt himsel'! It would no' happen to me, of course, I have a Gymnastic Trainer's Qualification."

I felt a story coming on so I turned and looked interested, knowing we were in for an impromptu tea break and eager to have managerial approval for a skive.

"Oh, ey! I was in the Olympic Team as a Trainer..." he didn't clarify which Olympics, "...but I had te pull out due to an injury." He didn't explain why a trainer would need to pull out with an injury either!

"I run a club now, teaching youngsters just up the road."

"Show us some moves then, Jim!" heckled Russ.

"Oh no, I'm too old now..." he shook his head with an old fellah wink "...but in ma younger days, I tell ye, I was shaggin' this girl up in Glasgow, married she was, lived in one of those flats with a courtyard and

Chapter 14 - Shifting Apart

flats directly opposite and either side, ye know what I am talkin' about?"

"What the fuck has this got to do with Gymnastics?" Andy interrupted.

"Just hang on a wee minute I'm getin tee it" he replied as Andy sat on the edge of the desk nearby.

"Well she used to put the latch down on the lock so her hubby's key would no be able to open the door if he came back unexpected, ye know? Anyway, one day he did, and bugger if he wasnee the biggest fucker in the world! So I pulled ma trousers on as quick as I could and grabbed ma stuff..." Jim built up the story with a few visual enactments "I started to hop on one foot, trying to get me shoe on at the same time as pulling up me trousers, and fell out the windy!!"

"How high up were you, Jim?" Andy questioned pretending to be startled.

"Oh, about SEVEN stories!" emphasis on the seven "Anyway, that saved me because there were washin' lines from house to house so I bounced from one te the other. By the time I got te the bottom I was fully dressed, landing on ma feet, hands in pocket walking off as if nothin' had happened."

"Fuckin' amazin'Jim! You are fuckin' amazin'!" I said sarcastically, Jim smiled appreciating the applause but not reading between the lines.

"Fuckin' Hell, Jim! Ya must 'ave been a folk hero up there!" Andy offered with more disguised sarcasm.

"Oh ey! That fuckin' big tart over there wouldne of lasted five minutes!" Jim indicated to Russ who replied with his middle finger.

"So, you were the top man, then?" I pushed keen for the tea break to continue.

"The 'Glasgow Blade' they called me in ma youth..."

Jim was just flowing "...many a time we'd meet, ma gang and other gangs that is..." chest puffing out "...I'd fight their top man wi' me switch blade. Never lost!" Jim puffed his chest out to its fullest trying to look the hard man.

"Fuckin' 'ell! Like in West Side Story, Jim?" I was blatant now, but Jim was too lost in fantasy to realise.

"Oh ey. A little, Davey, but it was REAL rough, no' glamorous!"

"La la la la la America, La la la la la America..." Russ gave his best 'West Side Story'.

"Ah fuck off! You wouldne even know where it was on the map!" Jim waved Russell's input away. "Anyhow, I had the pick of the girls and shagged 'em all except one 'cos she had a fanny like a bucket. I used te take her out in ma car and do all the oral stuff, ye know, but she'd satisfy hersel' by lowerin' hersel' onto ma gearstick." Jims visual display was a tad disturbing. "She was so keen, she took the fuckin' varnish off it after a while!"

"What was her name, Jim?"

"Buffy, I think!" He answered with such speed it was difficult to tell if he wasn't bull shitting for the first time in living history "Anyhow, what did I come in here for?"

Tea break over!

"Oh yeah, can ye work over, Neal and Alan have both phoned in sick so we're short on the afternoon shift."

"What's up with 'em, Jim?" Andy enquired.

"I dinny know, but somethin's no' right with 'em both off at the same time!" He shrugged his shoulders and went on his merry way.

Exactly one week later Neal and Alan returned on the same day and to our surprise both had healthy suntans! Now, bearing in mind we had a mild week of weather during their absence, this was some achievement!

Oh, and there was the small matter of a football

Chapter 14 - Shifting Apart

tournament in Portugal their team had planned to go to! Needless to say, they denied this scandalous accusation, stating that they had shared a sun-bed as part of their 'rehabilitation'.

"Son, ye could cure cancer with the amount of fuckin' radiation ye would need for that tan in five days ye lyin' shower o' bastards!" was one of Jim's 'back to work welfare inputs.'

After a couple of months with the new crew, I got the call to attend the forklift training school so I would be able to unload material as well as book it into the computer system. This new policy caused a lot of animosity as it was seen as a way of reducing personnel. I saw it as common sense taking into account the amount of down time we had between loads. It's probably fair to say that, along with Gaz Lee, a few others probably would have been better off without their licences, and we all would have been a lot safer!

The 'Old West Road Receiving Deck' where I spent many sleepy hours!

CHAPTER 15

DEMOLITION MEN

"It tay ma fuckin' fault."
[Russ]

The sound of the guard made him pause, and wait, as silent as a cat stalking his prey. Watching and waiting. He hugged the line of the building shrouded in darkness. If you blinked you would miss him amongst the shadows. He moved on, in through the door, closing in on his prey.

The group were sat at the table playing cards, talking noisily under the sheer light above them, shrouded in cigarette smoke not noticing the silent warrior creeping through the darkness around them.

Silently he approached his prey...closer...closer... close enough to hear him breathe. Moving one hand to the back of his head and the other level with his chin, with one movement his target's neck would be broken...

"WWWWWWWWWAAAAAAAAAAAAAAA!"

"Neal, put the fuckin' kettle on, eh?"

Geordie didn't even flinch in response to Neal's simulated attack.

"Ya didn't see me till the last minute did ya?" Neal boasted.

Neal nodded his head with a look of success on his face as he filled the kettle. We had all been the subject of one of Neal's simulated 'Ninja' attacks at some point, but Geordie was a regular target. He was a new lad on their shift and a good target for ribbing. We had Russ, they had Geordie.

Neal was a real character, apart from his kung fu. He

was a very slight male and was constantly ribbed about how feminine his hands were, and in fairness they were the hands of someone who had never picked up a shovel in his life. One thing that Neal did have, apart from a magnetic personality, was a huge cock! How did we all know this? It was because most of us had been exposed to it at some point, that's why! Such was his reputation for prominence in the trouser department that even our black comrades gave him respect.

Sitting with your back to Neal was a real mistake, as he would sneak up behind you and place his huge donga on your shoulder and leave it there until you noticed. Poor Barry was terrified of him or 'it' as is probably more to the point. He was a particular favourite target of Neal due to this obvious reaction.

Barry once made the mistake of leaving his pot of yoghurt on the office table, only to come back to find Neal dipping his old fellah into it.

"It helps with me thrush, Barry!" Neal explained.

I overcame the problem by warning Neal that if he came near me, I would grab a hold and take him for a walk around the track by it.

"How's that lad of yours doin', Alan?" Jim asked as he got up from the card table.

"Not too bad, he's been doin' a bit of extra work."

Alan's lad had been auditioned along with hundreds of other hopefuls to work on Kids TV and had been successful. He was about nine or ten at the time and his antics were a source of cheerful conversation whenever Alan was about.

Alan told us a story of how he took his lad to watch a Sunday league Match, so they could watch the local Pub side. Focused on the game Alan began to notice that

Chapter 15 - Demolition Men

a group of spectators were cheering, but not watching the game. He then saw his lad in an adjoining field bareback riding a horse! Not bad for a city boy! Alan shouted for him to get off, and this he did - dismounting with a backflip to the cheers of the crowd.

"I've done a wee bit of acting mysel' over the years…" the inevitability of Jim's comment was, at times, painful.

"You ever been in a film or on the telly then, Jim?" Sugar asked.

"Well, no' anythin' special. Mainly theatre and the like, but I was an extra in the film 'Spartacus'.''

There was a stunned silence for a second as we looked at each other. Even in the realms of Jim's fantasy world there had been limits. But to throw Kirk fucking Douglas into the pot was a biggie and was open to all manner of doubt, surely even in Jim's mind.

"What? You mean the Kirk Douglas film?" I enquired.

"Ey, that's the one." He confirmed.

"Who did ya play?" Alan asked with a smirk.

"Oh I was just an extra in a coupla scenes. I played a Roman Soldier" Jim clarified as casual and as a matter of fact as you like.

"I've see that film a few times, Jim. Which bit were ya in?" I forced his hand and saw his eyes darting around looking for an answer.

"I was near the start. There's a column of Roman soldiers, and I'm carrying one of those poles with the eagle on the top."

"A standard?" I tried to clarify.

"No, no. I was an extra! I'm in it for about 5-10 seconds. No' very long!"

"How did ya manage that ya fuckin' lyin' bastard?" Andy always questioned Jim's honesty.

"It was a friend of mine who knew one of the Casting

Directors. I gotta free week in Italy!"

"Was it made in Italy?" I didn't know, but enjoyed watching Jim work.

"No, no, not all, but that bit was!"

I bow to the Master Bull-shitter I thought.

"Davey, you're drivin' course has been brought forward so ye can go on Monday mornin', OK son?"

"Ye lucky bastard! I wish I could do mine again. It was a doddle!" Geordie said enviously.

"Just watch out for Baby Face." Russ added.

"Who the fuck is Baby Face?" I asked.

"Oh, you'll see!" Geordie answered.

"WWWWWWWWAAAAAAAAAA!" Neal broke Geordie's spine with a punch to the lower back.

"Ya didn't even know I was there did ya!!!"

Monday morning, 9 o'clock and I arrived at the forklift-training centre which was a small affair and could be described as a big garage at best! An internal 'pent' style shed with a partition wall separated the students from the instructors. It wasn't long before I met Baby Face, but didn't use the nickname as I was warned it could affect my pass or failure of the course.

If you can imagine one of those very cheap plastic dolls from the bargain shops, then bring to mind the face. Well, that was what was standing in front of us telling us about health and safety. Oh yeah, and add some small buckteeth to the picture with some immaculate wispy blonde shoulder length hair, mullet style. His overalls were pressed with turned up collar and cuffs. Add gold chains, rings and bracelets, and you should have your image completed.

You would think that such a flamboyant appearance would lend to a matching personality. On the contrary, he spoke in monotone with a character to match. His fellow

Chapter 15 - Demolition Men

instructor was Phil, who was very ordinary looking in comparison, and had a minor speech impediment which prevented him from pronouncing his 'R's. This didn't stop him from shouting out his instructions during tests, although it could be quite off-putting.

"Wight! I want you to lift that fowe by fowa pallet wight up to the top of that stack. Weverse, come wight back and wemembato check the wea at all times. Weady? Pwoceed!"

As much as he was an excellent teacher, it was difficult to wemain (sorry) remain composed, especially on the final drive. My two co-trainees and myself managed to pass our tests on both 'sit and reach' and 'counterbalance' trucks even with Phil's R-less directions, and it was on this day whilst awaiting our results that a strange thing happened as I walked into the canteen for breakfast.

Walking along the road between buildings I became aware of a peddy truck coming towards me, going downhill with a white 30-something chap at the wheel. He was travelling at a fair speed so I purposely hugged the building line to stay out of the way.

To his left and my right was a pile of plastic crates and wooden pallets stacked up and empty. For whatever reason, he went straight into them with such force that he flipped over the top of the wheel of his truck in a contorted fashion and landed with a yelp into the said pile of empties.

I ran towards him at a pace, concerned that he was really hurt, and as I reached him he was just getting up. Before I could open my mouth he looked at me like a scared cat and proceeded to sprint away, leaving the mess behind, along with his truck? Well, what do you do? So I did what every concerned employee would do, I went and had my sandwich. On the way back, the truck was gone and the stack was back as it was pre-collision. Had I imagined it? I didn't say anything because, well, there was nothing to say!

We had an early finish that day because it was Friday [of course!] having received our licences and pass certificates. I was eager to return to the deck on Monday morning to practice my new found skills and drive some of the many assorted machines available to me now.

Training on a nice, shiny, well-maintained truck was a far cry from the skips-on-wheels in use on the deck, that were in use pretty much 24-hours a day. You had to be doubly careful to avoid mechanical failure, and I was to discover this the hard way.

'The Tank' was an 8-ton monster counterbalance truck with power steering. It could travel at a fair speed and could lift pretty much anything it was tasked to do, unlike its smaller counterparts. Being the modest type, I decided that the Tank would be my first operational drive, and I jumped on at the first opportunity and set off with verve. 'Easy money' I thought as I shipped and unloaded pallets, and it wasn't long before I was taking a nice, casual approach, totally ignoring all the rules of the operator's manual now located at the bottom of my locker. Back and forth I went, fully laden with pallets, to different store areas until the road deck was completely empty and I decided to park up for the end of the shift.

I drove towards the small office to see Leroy. He was walking over to the main office to make the first brew of his 2pm-10pm shift. I intended to stop the truck out the front of the small road receiving office, so I lowered the forks in anticipation and applied the brakes. Nothing! Harder! Still Nothing! Handbrake on! Still nothing!

"OH SHIT!!!!!!" I shouted as on I went with nothing to stop me other than the biggest thing in front of me.

Chapter 15 - Demolition Men

My forks went under the crash barrier outside the office and began to make two large holes in the metal panels, pushing the bottom in and the top out. With an almighty bang the body of the truck hit the barrier, and I was thrown over the steering wheel into the upright forks, fortunately cushioning the blow with my head!

"BASTARD!!!!!" I screamed as my head spun and I was thrown back into my seat.

After the initial shock, I noticed that I had attracted an audience of onlookers, clapping and cheering. I looked at the crash barrier which was still upright, then the small office that was still standing.

Right!, I thought, *Weverse!* So I did, slowly pulling the forks out and not building up too much speed so the truck would roll to a standstill, *just that last bit* I thought. The office thankfully appeared to be okay.

With an unwanted grinding noise followed by a creak and a groan, half the ceiling tiles fell in and years of dust and associated shit that had built up in the roof space descended into the office, covering the computer terminal, printer, desk, chair and newspaper that Leroy had been reading just moments before.

"Shit! Fuck! Bollocks! Bastard!" I said angrily to myself.

"Hey, Leroy!" Andy shouted. "Have you seen the new décor in ye office?"

Leroy appeared at the door, mug in hand, paused momentarily to observe, and without a word walked over to his workstation. He stood at the door looking in, shaking his head. He looked back at me and said "Wonka!" still shaking his head.

As I watched, he coolly lifted his paper, dusted down his work area and sat down, laying his paper on the desk again, and reading as he sipped his tea.

Never again did I allow complacency to creep into my truck driving, unlike others who never learned! Russ was awarded a licence just before me, and was the loudest laugh during my little accident. But it wasn't long before his antics began and became increasingly bigger and more dangerous.

Pallets that held the side frames of a car were the favourite of the train forklift drivers due to their large size. Filling empty space quicker meant a quicker turnaround of trucks and trains leading to longer break times. Each pallet could hold 15 sides, so were car length and about 6feet tall and 8 feet wide. On each bottom corner was a ball, with a hollow on each top corner for the ball to slot into. This meant they could be stacked easily. An experienced driver could carry 3 stacked if he wanted to get an early lunch or dinner.

One day Russell decided to carry them 4, high, against all the advice of the other drivers. His truck was not built to carry the weight, so the rear wheels bounced up and down as he carried the pallets to the roller doors. He had about 2 inches to spare as he came through, but the slight ramp reduced this gap causing the top pallet to catch the doors and wedge the tower in with the truck below. Common sense would suggest you stop and re-evaluate the situation, agreed? Not Russ. On went the gas, and brute force was his answer to this 'minor' problem.

As the top pallet was scraped through the gap it began to lift, along with the pallet below, out of the hollows. This gave a 'crocodile mouth' effect. By this time I had stopped what I was doing and watched with open mouth. Tyres spun and rubber burnt as the tower was forced through and the mouth of the crocodile got wider. The final few inches of pallet came through the door and the mouth closed, unfortunately not back into the holes, and as they

Chapter 15 - Demolition Men

slammed back down, the weight lifted the truck off the floor throwing Russ forward and lifting the rear balls out of the top two pallets.

It was at this moment that Mickey 'Gringo' Graham came round the corner on his twentieth cup of coffee to see what the noise was. Almost simultaneously, Russ's efforts to defy gravity failed and the two tons of pallet came crashing to the ground directly towards Gringo.

"Look out Mick!" I screamed at the top of my voice.

By the Grace of God he heard me and in one swift movement his legs gave way and he scrambled out of reach of the falling metal.

As the smoke cleared, Mick ran towards Russ, coffee still in hand (with not a drop spilt!). He bestowed a tirade of expletives too numerous to mention at Russ, to which Russ replied: "It ain't my fault if the pallets am SHIT!"

In his first month as a driver, Russ even managed to derail the train when he hit it so hard with his forklift. This was a feat only ever equalled by Tipper! His antics caused much concern to all around, especially the top floor gaffers who realised he had used the entire year's budget for repairs in six weeks. He even ran over someone's foot! How he never killed anyone is one of life's great mysteries.

His reputation became legend amongst the delivery drivers who would cringe if he was unloading them due to his uncanny ability to rip pretty much every curtain that ever came into the factory! He did calm down eventually as the novelty wore off and the number of incidents became so great that even he couldn't ignore them.

The peddy trucks were by far the best fun to drive, especially if you had free rein to do the factory coffee machine tour. A full battery would give good speed and they were fantastic on corners! Mick made one his own due to the strain on his back caused by the 200 miles

Living in a Plant

of walking a day round the factory. I would occasionally whiz around delivering plastic boxes of parts with Mac on the back, hands on my shoulders. I think he fancied himself as a bit of a surfer. Once our work was done we would head for the quiet of the Old West to enjoy a natter with the crew down there.

Built on a slope, the Old West had many steep runways into different parts of the plant which were easily negotiable when the ground was dry. But years of use and little maintainance had given some of the concrete floors a smooth finish that would hold the frost and the wet turning it into a skid pan. I found this out to my cost one chilly morning as Mac and I headed off for our breakfast.

The flat areas were not a problem, but as we turned into the entry to the main factory we began to descend towards the large clear rubber doors which greeted you as you entered the building. I applied the brakes, which locked the wheels perfectly, but we continued to slide at the same speed and direction into the wall and crash barrier!

"NO BRAKES!" I shouted, thinking this to be the case, and Mac immediately dismounted sliding to a halt with all the coolness of an acrobat. I tried to turn the truck to no avail, and it increased speed. So I jumped off. Not being as cool as Mac and hitting the ground running, on ice, going downhill, I felt my legs turn, unable to stop and headed straight for the doors which slowed me down. Alas they allowed me to continue through so that I landed face down on the floor inside the building. I got up and limped back to the truck to see Mac, unruffled, standing next to the dented and buzzing peddy truck.

"Nice parkin' Dave!" He said, followed by a deep loud laugh.

Of course, we reported the incident immediately!

Chapter 15 - Demolition Men

Well, we parked it up outside Mick's office and denied any knowledge in actual fact.

I witnessed the accidents and aftermath of many major and minor collisions by the majority of drivers, but the King without doubt, was Tipper. Tipper had no idea about safety. If you got in his way, tough shit! When the train came in, his job was to unload it and backfill it as quickly as possible, and not being the brightest button in the box, safety was of no consequence. He would have regarded injury as collateral damage if he had known what it meant.

Russ took a little of the heat off him, but when they were together unloading the train, you dared not walk the train deck. Those that did, didn't again! Those that didn't know, soon learned as pallets crashed and banged in every direction.

Tipper once hit a crash barrier so hard that he bent the body of his truck so that the roof could not be properly aligned and was subsequently written off! No mean feat, because the trucks were tough little workers. They needed to be!

A large, expensive piece of machinery lived just at the rear of the train deck and occasionally would require a driver from the train to empty it. The route into it was small and you had to use all your skills to unload it, including a lot of patience to reload it with an empty pallet.

Tipper was sent just prior to his dinner break, so his patience was already waiting in the queue at the canteen.

The first we got to know about the incident was when an irate track gaffer came onto the deck.

"What fukin' retard did you send to unload it then?" I overheard him ask Mick.

"Tipper went. Why?" Mick asked.

Living in a Plant

"Because..." he replied pronouncing every letter, "...THE FUCKIN' TWAT HAS CAUSED A TRILLION POUNDS WORTH OF DAMAGE...THAT'S WHY!" and a Trillion pounds was a lot of money in those days.

"What? Unloading one pallet? Nah! Can't be! It must have been an overheat or somethin'," Mick surmised.

"Oh yeah!" the gaffer paused and pointed at a truck coming up the deck. "What's that then?"

Tipper held his polystyrene box full of pie and chips under his arm, and had a look of impending pleasure on his face. On top of the uprights of his forks, without his knowledge, was a big red sign:

'DO NOT LIFT BEYOND THIS POINT'

Conclusive evidence methinks.

Probably the best evidence of Tipper's mental vacancy was a story that was legendary amongst the work force. It all began one day when Tipper, as usual, was loading the train with empties.

A large group of managers were walking up through the stores looking at things talking shite and pointing as they went. As they made their way along the train deck, Tipper, in a rush as usual and thinking about whatever Tipper thinks about, was stacking the pallets in anticipation of the train's arrival. At the time of the incident, Tipper was driving along with a large Metro Side pallet, which is of a fair size. Going in reverse is not a problem as your visibility is unobstructed, but going forward you had to be especially careful, clearing the way in advance as you approached.

The entire group saw him coming except for one, who was sent flying by the impact of the pallet against his body. He landed in a crumpled heap on the train track which was a 5 foot drop!

Fortunately, the poor chap sustained no serious

Chapter 15 - Demolition Men

injury, but the incident was deemed serious enough for Tipper to be interviewed by a senior manager to consider disciplinary action. From what I heard, it went something like this:

"So, Robert," (Tipper's real name) "just give me your date of birth for the form."

Impatient sigh as Tipper tried to look as if he was unconcerned about the incident.

"Now tell me what happened please Robert."

"I was just gooin along when I saw the bloke, heard a bang and saw the bloke fly onto the track!"

"What?" the manager enquired surprised, "you saw him before you hit him?"

"Oh Yeah!" Tipper replied.

"So, why didn't you stop?"

"Well, I was in a rush and he shoulda got out of the way quicka!"

"Robert, I am challenged by your unique point of view..." with sarcasm, "but the fact remains that you saw him. So if that was the case, why didn't you give an audible warning as per your training?"

Tipper looked puzzled by the question, "why didn't I what?"

"Your horn, your fuckin' horn..." slight loss of control but quickly regrouped "...sorry, why didn't you sound your horn to let him know you were coming?"

"I didn't want to startle 'im!"

"So, you thought you would run him over instead ye fukin' chimpanzee?"

"Tay my fault! He shoulda got out of the way!!" Tipper protested.

"Any connection between your reality and the reality of the human race is a pure coincidence, isn't it Robert?"

"Eh?" confused look.

"Thank you Robert, you can be rest assured that all the necessary action will be taken" he said with conviction. "That will be all."

You will be surprised to hear that no disciplinary action followed, (or not, perhaps?)

All humour aside, I was always amazed by the amount of close calls we had, and that was just in the area I worked, and those I witnessed elsewhere. It was a dangerous place, and often the safety of the individual was cast aside in the name of production. 'Keep the Line Moving!'

I got to know a chap who was a little older than me, with two kids, just like I have. I worked on his crew a few times and played a few games of football in the same side on Saturday afternoons. I remember his name, but wouldn't use it out of respect. He went to work one day at 2pm and following a work-related accident, died before the end of his shift. I will always remember him.

'Nuff said.

Crash Alley; the road to forklift training!

CHAPTER 16

A BIT ABOUT MINE

"Ahgowayourda!"
[Mudder]

It was Friday May 22nd 1992 when I finally tied the knot with Tracy, and we did it in style on Kings Norton Green in a very old church. 140 friends and family attended a gloriously sunny day at the ceremony, followed by food, beer, disco and karaoke at Harbourne Golf Club. A great day and night followed by two weeks in Orlando, Florida where Tracy's illusion of 'it'll be just like Alton Towers' was finally shattered.

After just a few years in our new house, Tracy's aspirations to buy an old and run down house to renovate could not be bridled anymore, and as usual we needed more space to plan for the future. I suppose it came to a head when I attempted to fit a new set of taps to our bathroom suite in the two bedroom box we were living in. Sink taps and washers were not a problem, but the bath/shower mixer was a different proposition. The problem was that the bathroom was so small that you could, in one movement, hoist yourself off the toilet seat and straight into the bath. This meant that the space to work in when fitting the mixer was very, very limited.

I refused to be defeated, and managed to remove the old taps with relative ease. I then proceeded to position the new set in the same holes, now left vacant. I squeezed myself between the bath and toilet, working my body into the cavity, using double joints that I didn't know I had! With the skill of a true professional, I tightened the bolts and the job was done.

As explained, getting into the cavity wasn't too much of a problem. What I had not planned for was my body swelling as I got hot from the exertion. As I attempted to reverse my way out I found I was unable to move! At one point my elbow was touching below the back of my neck and at another, my face was pressed against the toilet bowl with my mouth within millimetres of the underside of the seat! Now I don't care how much in touch you are with your own body, but having your mouth that close to an area where I had previously emptied my bowels was a very disturbing experience!

Struggle on I did, but to no avail. Eventually sheer exhaustion overcame me and I slumped back, catching my breath. Where was Tracy? Well, she had popped out for 5 minutes to 'get a bit of shopping' and we all know what that means, don't we?

I cried out a couple of times, but only "Anja" our dog came and proceeded to stick her tongue in my face and mouth and seemed to enjoy my inability to fight her off. Not being the smartest of dogs, she didn't understand my pleas for her to "Go and get help! Tell the Sheriff Dave's got stuck behind the shitter!" To cut a very long story short, after about an hour of relaxing and deep breathing to calm me down, I eased my way out. This left me with a permanent reminder in the shape of a neck injury that comes back to haunt me when the weather gets cold or if I'm alone in a bathroom shop.

It is probably fair to say that my family has a history of self-generated idiocy, not that we are a bunch of thickies, but we seem to do things like this on occasion. My parents are Irish, so this has a tendency to make the incidents even more comical. Take, for instance, the time my mom went to a posh Indian restaurant with her sister

Chapter 16 - A Bit About Mine

and brother-in-law.

The starters and main meal finished, the waiter placed three small dishes with a hot steaming rolled-up towel on each side plate, for wiping hands (obviously!). Not seeing the like before, mom decides that this must be dessert and proceeds to take a bite! "Fuckin' hell! Dat's tough!" she exclaimed to everyone's amazement and amusement.

One quirk she shares with moms across the nation is her inability to answer the phone without sounding like the 'Lady of the Manor'. For years we waited to get a phone due to the cost in the early eighties. Finally we did, and how happy were we when the cream coloured 'dog and bone' arrived and took pride of place on the purpose built shelf created by Dad. The only problem was my brother Derek and I had to have a level one security pass to use it and Mom would wave her hands around frantically in an 'I'm not here' fashion every time it rang. I of course would always oblige her by smiling and saying "yep! She is right here in front of me."

Imagine the look on your kids faces if you put one of those dial pad locks on the home phone or a mock up type on their mobiles! Kids of today eh!

Dad's best trick is the ability to be able to choke on pretty much anything edible. We have had to put up with this trait for years! At any given moment during a meal, he would jump up and have to shove his fingers down his throat to fetch out a piece of unchewed something-or-other.

This habit of his died a death following an incident at home, when he was munching on a delicious piece of steak at the kitchen table and decided to start retching. Panicking, Mom ran and shouted to my brother, Derek, who was home for a couple of days, telling him that Dad was choking! By the time Derek got to him, Dad was in the back garden coughing after managing to remove the offending piece of meat. Unfortunately for Dad, Derek thought he was still choking, so he grabbed him around the chest and proceeded to try to remove the blockage with the Heimlich manoeuvre. Derek, being some three stone heavier and a weight lifter, threw poor old Dad around like a rag doll. He was trying to speak, but only managed to gasp, and Derek perceived this to be further choking and began hitting Dad in the middle of his back with some force. Eventually he managed to escape Derek's grip and backed himself into the corner, putting his hands up to prevent being first-aided to death!

Whilst Derek was punching the shit out of Dad, Mom in a fit of temper, picked up the offending steak and launched it down the garden. It was closely followed by the cat that disappeared over the back fence with it. Funnily enough, Dad takes care to chew his food more thoroughly now.

Anyway, after the toilet incident I thought I would never attempt DIY again. How wrong I was. The house we decided to buy was a 1902 end terrace that needed 'a bit of love and affection' according to the estate agent. "More like a fuckin' good shaggin!" I exclaimed when I first saw it. But we purchased it nevertheless as I owed it to Tracy who had supported me without question when my business went down the pan in our earlier life together.

We were both working full time and money was plentiful, allowing us to do lots of modernising which I enjoyed about as much as slicing my balls with a Stanley knife. Unlike my Dad who had to be physically restrained on occasions due to his annoying habit of drilling holes in things, including our brand new central heating pipes! Being such an old house, it had the tendency to give people the creeps, including Tracy, who wanted it in the

Chapter 16 - A Bit About Mine

first place, and her sister Melanie. Melanie refused to stay at night unless all the lights were left on.

Not that I'm a sceptic or anything, but coming from an Irish Roman Catholic background, I was buried under stories of ghosts and ghouls and wailing banshees from friends and relatives.

These were topped up with stories from the priests and nuns, of Hell and Damnation, and an eternity in Purgatory if you didn't eat all your cabbage.

My Grandmother on my mother's side was subject to an incident which came about from her fear of the Dark side. These were made worse when you live in the middle of nowhere in deepest, darkest County Wexford. She had to go and visit some old lady or something as one of her daily duties (I'm sure I will be corrected) and had to ride home on her pushbike through the dark lanes. For some reason, a ditch was dug at the side of the road, which was about 5 feet deep. She didn't see it as she was busy looking out for the banshee that might be following her, and in she went! Being only 4feet 10 inches tall, she disappeared from view.

Living in a supposedly enlightened world, we would accept this as an accident and probably try to find the hole digger so he could be sued for compensation. But in my Granny's young world full of demons and devils, she convinced herself that she had been swallowed up by Hell itself, managed to scramble out of her hole, and ran home in a state of hysteria. Not unlike a banshee herself. (Have I finally solved the banshee mystery?).

These superstitions were passed down to her family, and my mother who still has a little of the inbred fear of the church and what it could do to you if you were a bad follower.

I'll never forget the time the local Parish Priest came

to see us when we moved house. He marched around the house as if he owned it, criticising her for not having any religious pictures or symbols on the walls and sideboards. I would have described the scene as a naughty child being patronised by an adult. Cheeky Bastard!

Her true fears were brought to the fore when I was sixteen and an older cousin who came over on the boat with Mom and Dad from Ireland in the sixties, died prematurely. He died in the early hours and almost simultaneously, so Mom says, she was being tugged out of the bed by some invisible force that was calling her name. With Dad being on nights and no one else in the house, she was terrified and rightly so under the circumstances. She convinced herself that my cousin was trying to contact her as he was going over to the 'other side'. In addition to the invisible force, the phone began to ring at the same time. This was the little detail she couldn't explain. Why would the phone ring at the time of his death?

"Well, ya know what it is?" my sick juvenile mind working overtime as she told me the story.

"What?" she asked innocently.

"Hells Bells!" I replied in my best horror movie voice.

Well, you can imagine, she hit a thousand feet and it took all the reassurance that I could muster to bring her back down to earth.

As usual, I went out the next night on the piss, but for some unknown reason I came back early, about 11.30pm, a little worse for wear with drink. Up the road I stumbled, the street being quiet and dark. I began to make out a bright light in the near distance where our house should have been. As I got nearer I realised it was our house.

"What the f...?"

I quickened my pace, stopping at the end of the path, looking at our semi-detached house. Every light in the

Chapter 16 - A Bit About Mine

house was on, and all the curtains were open. The bloke on nights at the National Grid must have wondered what was going on as our house had a warm glow all around it. I shielded my eyes as I opened the door.

"Is dat you Dave?" Mom shouted from upstairs.

"No!" I replied.

"Come up here quick!" she didn't believe me, so I staggered up the stairs.

"What's going on, Mom?" I slurred, and saw her lying...in my bed! Rosary beads were tightly gripped in her hand and every religious symbol we possessed sat on the bedside table.

"You can sleep in my bed tonight," she said, frantically.

Dad was on nights so there was no chance of him coming home in a drunken stupor and mistaking me for Mom. Could you imagine? AAAARRRGGHHH!

So, too pissed to argue, I slept, with a thick sweater on my head to block out the light.

The following morning I sat at the breakfast table.

"Well?" Mom looked at me expectantly.

"Well, What?"

"Did anything happen?" she pushed.

"Oh, fuck me! Yeah!" I was hit round the head with a plastic spoon.

"Don't fuckin' curse!" I was warned.

"Well. I was asleep about half an hour, then..." I stuffed a mouthful of Cornflakes in.

"Yes? Yes?" she said impatiently.

"...then I felt somethin' pullin' my leg." I finished.

"Jesus and Mary!" she crossed herself.

"Just like I'm pullin' yours now," I laughed loudly.

"You little fucker"; ironic comment really since I was a foot taller and four stone heavier!

My brother, Derek, reckons that something happened

to him when he slept in Mom's bed, but I think he was taking the piss really. It was a while before she got back in her own bed, and even longer before the lights went out again.

Tracy's family are a very religious bunch. Her Mom, Sue, was a practising Christadelphian, very much involved in the church on a daily basis. Her Dad, Rodney, was a 6feet 5-inch big personality, man's man, who was the image of Hank Marvin, glasses and all.

Her Mom and Dad had a rocky marriage, going from a fairly affluent environment to bankruptcy, having to move from house to house. Rod was a big drinker so this compounded the problem, Sue turning to the church for help and courage.

During their period of bankruptcy, Rod went from job to job as an insurance broker, trying to get back on his feet. Visiting people's houses, he needed a car, and only being able to afford a few hundred quid, the array of different motors he bought and sold was a scream! The best one was a 'Vauxhall Victor Estate', his being the only one I have ever seen then and since. On one occasion he had no wheels due to him breaking down in his Skoda, so he borrowed our car which was a cherry pink (Tracy's idea) Mini 1000 with bucket seats and alloy wheels.

Now, I'm 5 feet 10 inches, and found it cramped. Rod just looked ridiculous! At 6feet 5 inches and 17 stone, crammed into the seat with a knee either side of his ear. I think he got a few whistles whilst driving, but he loved the attention. Fortunately for him, it wasn't raining as 'Timmy the Mini' (again not my idea) wasn't very waterproof, allowing a lot, well all, the rain into the footwells. So much so, that I had to take my shoes and socks off when driving. Tracy cried her eyes out when we sold it. I didn't!

Chapter 16 - A Bit About Mine

Rod was one of those blokes that you met and never forgot. Loud and brash, he was a big cricket and football fan, spending as much of his time at Villa Park as a steward, then down to Edgbaston for the cricket season. Because of his many contacts, I received many free tickets to different games and usually ended up in the same hospitality suite. In 1987 he got me a one-day only job at Edgbaston Cricket Ground. I was to be the doorman in the lounge where all the celebrities sat during the "Rainforest Cricket Match".

Taking part were many British actors including 'Damo' from Brookside (before he got stabbed, remember him?), Paul Young (an idol of Tracy's - who was there with me - but didn't pluck up the courage to speak to him), Donny Osmond (another idol of Tracy's from a different era) and Gary Mason (British Heavyweight Champion – and I was looking after him...yeah, right!). Probably the best of the bunch and the biggest thrill to meet was Bill Wyman who had turned up with two 18-year-old identical twins. Bleach-blonde, the twins that is, and gorgeous, and he was probably doing them both! Lucky Bastard!

The 'Hooray Henries' running the show were all jump suited up and wearing earpieces with walkie-talkies, dashing around and giving out orders. Some of them were so far up the arses of the celebs that only the 'NIKE' symbols on the bottom of their trainers were showing! Anyway, I got to look like Kevin Costner for a day, and wound up the 'Henries' who didn't have the correct door passes: "NO PASS? YOU'RE NOT COMING IN THEN!"

Fantastic!

Rod had a full social life; I think mainly due to the fact that he was surrounded by women in his home life, he needed to get away. He enjoyed nothing more than to put his feet up and read his paper in quiet, calm surroundings which he rarely found at home. One of the biggest (literally) disruptions were his mother-in-law, known as Margaret, Marian and Polly - I never knew what to call her! She was 25 stone and wasn't very mobile.

When she went for dinner at Christmas or other special occasions, the dogs (Shane and Tara) would scarper in case they were trodden on or kicked by her huge legs. Rod would look up at me slyly from behind his newspaper with a 'look at the fuckin' size of that' expression on his face. Going to the toilet for her was a bit of an effort which could reduce us both to fits. 5 minutes to cross the living room, 10 minutes to get half way up the stairs, then:

"Too late," she would say and down she would come for a change of underwear in the kitchen.

It must be an old lady thing. They just insist on showing off their underwear at any and every opportunity! I once saw half a dozen well-endowed old ladies climbing over a 12-inch tall picket fence from a car park, herding towards the Bingo Club in Redditch. Clutching out to each other, one fell over and the rest followed, whooping and laughing, legs thrown akimbo exposing large pants to the rest of the passersby.

I was never unfortunate enough to witness Tracy's Nan urinate on the stairs in our new house, mainly because she refused to come around due to the stairs being so steep, and the toilet being at the end of a long landing. In all fairness, when we moved in I wasn't overly keen myself! Big, old and cold it was.

"It's got character!" Tracy would say, usually when I was covered in muck, dust and shit, and feeling a little pissed off and ready to throw the towel in.

Working nights was a nightmare as I had to try to sleep in the day with the builders coming in and out. Strangely enough, it was one day when no one was

Chapter 16 - A Bit About Mine

working and I was in for my first undisturbed sleep that some spotty 16 year old decided to try and get in through a rear downstairs window. I awoke to the sound of the double glazed panel cracking, Anja still being asleep at the end of the bed. I jumped up and ran downstairs, cricket bat in hand, to be faced with this fucking spotty monkey looking at me though the window! Needless to say, I flipped!

I gave chase, not stopping to realise that I was dressed in only boxer shorts and vest. The youth had a bit of a start on me, but I was in good shape so made up the ground running parallel along the road as he went through the trees opposite our house.

My penis-retention system on the front of my boxers wasn't working too well, so out popped my old man waving frantically at passersby. Coming in the opposite direction was an old lady walking her Yorkie dogs. Not having the spotty offender in view, all she would have seen was me swinging my bat in the air, and my penis bouncing about in the wind. She picked up her dogs and turned around, trying desperately to quick-step away as I charged past her hurling abuse at the unseen offender. I've seen her since, but she didn't say much to me.

Anyway, I caught the youth and handed him over to the local constabulary. It later transpired that he had been in my neighbour's house too! As my adrenaline levels subsided I realised my nakedness and felt a little embarrassed surrounded by police officers. Worse was the unbelievable pain in the soles of my feet. I hadn't stopped to put any shoes on, which isn't a problem on the tarmac path and the grass, but the front drive was gravel! A few hours later, my feet swelled up and changed colour causing a three-day absence from work!

It is amazing how adrenaline can affect you in a

tense situation, especially when chasing someone or being chased. I found this out one summer when I spent a lot of my 16th year in London with my family.

Cousin Phillip and I, being of the same age, would spend our time playing darts, snooker, watching the Olympics and hanging around Central London looking for females to chat up. One afternoon, in the British Museum, we scored! Well, I did and she had a mate. We arranged to meet up that evening, and did so, going over to East Ham to meet the two young ladies. When we arrived, the friend had been replaced with my new girlfriend's older sister, and I suddenly became the unlucky one!

We hung out, drank beer and walked them home about 9pm, ending up behind a row of shops with apartments on top, in a dark alleyway. After exchanging our goodbyes (bet you never heard it called that before!) the girls walked up a flight of iron steps to one of the flats. I heard the giggles from the both of them all the way to the back door of the premise which opened with two shadows appearing in the background. Then, SMACK! The sound of skin on skin in a violent manner filled our ears followed by a loud male voice:

"Where the fack 'ave you been? Get in Naaaa!"

Phil and I looked at each other in the darkness, and at one point I thought to run up to save the damsel in distress. This thought lasted about half a second, when I realised I would be met by an angry Dad at the top of the stairs. Then:

"OI! You! Fackin' cam ere!"

The voice turned its attention to us, and with a clang as shoe hit metal on the stairs above us, we voiced a simultaneous: "OH SHIT!!"and off we went at speed, closely followed by the as yet unseen pursuer.

As we came to the end of the alleyway, the

Chapter 16 - A Bit About Mine

bright streetlight assisted our view of the escape route. Unfortunately, Phil's chosen route was in the opposite direction to mine and I immediately realised that it was Phil who knew where he was going, I didn't! My head, arms and body turned and began going in Phil's direction, but my legs decided to carry on the way I had initially chosen. This running style doesn't work, so the inevitable crash to the ground followed.

At this point it all became a bit of a blur, but Phil says that he had turned to see me, mid-flight, then hit the deck. He describes seeing me in one movement bounce into the air, legs turning as my feet hit the floor and take off, just avoiding the foot of our pursuer connecting with my body. To say that we ran like the clappers is an understatement. We ran the best part of a mile in about 5 minutes, and didn't stop until we reached the Thames.

A more mature mind would have told us that the "mad Dad" would have returned home by this time, satisfied that he had proved his fatherly prowess. However, being young and a little naïve, we were still convinced he was after us. So with this belief we carried on running, going through a subway-like tunnel under the Thames. I shit you not! It was the longest run I have ever made. The other end of this tunnel was a spot in the distance, and with our imagination working overtime, I was near to pissing myself. Still, we got back safely, and we laugh about the whole episode every time we see each other.

Good Days. Miss 'em!

Right, that's a bit more about mine, which could probably be another book, but I'll try and stay with the plot. So there we were, another new house, lots of money, newly married and I was pretty happy in my job...or was I?

CHAPTER 17

SICK AND RELIEF

*"Change is as good as a rest,
especially when you aint the one fucking changing."*

[Me]

"So, where did the bunny thing come from?"

"I'm not sure, Russ."

"And why an egg? Bunnies don't lay eggs...do they?"

Russ probed the theory behind Easter as we waited for our morning 'Team Meeting'.

"I suppose it represents new life, ya know, when Jesus rose from the dead. The egg is a new life thing, 'en it?" I surmised without having a clue what I was talking about.

"Naaa! Yem talking bollocks ye cunt!" Russ obviously didn't agree. "That's about as likely as the fukin' baggies [West Bromwich Albion] getting' in the Premier League!"

Well, what would *you* suggest? We eat chocolate babies? Or how about a nice fuckin' chocolate foetus?" I suggested with a little irritation in my voice.

"There aye no need to become belligerent," Russ looked quietly proud of himself that he got his new word into the conversation again.

"Fuckin' 'ell! Russ has swallowed a dictionary!" Tipper twitched.

At this point, in walked our team leader, Vaughn, or 'Lurch' as he was known due to being nearly seven feet tall[slight exaggeration] and not looking too dissimilar to his namesake from the "Adams family".

"Roight..." followed by right leg lift and deep fart, "18 on the train in about 15 minutes" we were briefed.

"Is that it?" Tipper twitched.

"Eh?" Vaughn looked shocked that Tipper had questioned him.

"Well, ya do the same thing every day! Ya come in, say 'Roight'" (in his best Vaughn), "...drop ya guts, say '18 on the train', and that's it! So why do we need to come here to be told that?"

We all sat in stunned silence at Tipper's attempt to question management with a reasonable, sound argument, and looked to Vaughn with anticipation.

"I don't! I sometimes say '15 on the train' after droppin' me guts." He turned to me, "Dave, Mickey Graham wants te see ya", and with that he walked out, followed by Tipper, twitching furiously which must have been a reaction to talking sense for more than five seconds.

I wandered down to the foreman's office.

"Alright, Mick" I greeted as Mick sat at his desk with Neal who was also a Team Leader by this time.

"Alroight, Dave!" Mick sipped his coffee. "We're de-manning [reducing staff in pre political correctness speak] on the deck, Dave, so I've got to let ya go. But you'll be goin' to Lloyd on the fifth aisle store as sick and relief, okay?"

"Why me?" I enjoyed my current job and didn't want to be moved.

"You've got the least service, Dave," was my only explanation.

"Service? Fuckin' Service? You've got half a dozen fuckin' mongs up there, but ya want to get rid of me?"

"It doesn't work like that, Dave. It's 'last in, first out'. Always has been."

The issue of service really got up my nose. I mean, you could have a superman and an idiot doing the same job, with Superman being ten times more productive. But

Chapter 17 - Sick and Relief

if he had one day's service less that the idiot, Superman was the first to go! I understood that this protected the less mentally fortunate, but surely you've got to have the best man (or woman) for the job so that productivity is good, as is profit, and the slower ones can be carried. At the time it was probably a too simplistic way of looking at it, but I was young and keen.

"Change is as good as a rest, eh Dave?" Russ tried to make me feel better.

"Well you fuckin' go then!" It didn't work.

"Eh, don't become bel..."

"Don't fuckin' say it Russ, just don't!" I warned with a finger and he didn't.

Barry placed a cup of tea in front of me and I calmed, because 'there ain't nothing that can't be solved with a cuppa!'

"Thanks, Barry" I smiled. "How's things on the blow-job front?" I decided a complete change of subject was the best remedy, and focus on someone else's problems.

"No. Nothin' yet" he replied with a sigh.

I must explain that Barry was attached to a lovely woman with a beautiful daughter. He had a great relationship with his partner due to them both loving shopping as much as each other. Unfortunately, and to his utter dismay, he couldn't get her to partake of the pleasures of oral sex.

"I'd just shove it in 'er mouth when she's asleep!" Russ lifted his head from 'The Daily Sport' – his favourite read.

"Yeah, you probably would!" I retorted sarcastically.

"Eh?" Russ was unsure if I was being sarcastic or not.

"I just day know how to get round it, Dave! I scrub it so it's clean, an' I've even said I'll put somethin' on it like honey or somethin' so it tastes nice. But she day wanna know!" Barry looked dejected.

"Well, have you tried swingin' ye arse round when yem givin' 'er a muff-dive?" Russ couldn't help himself.

"I 'ave, but she just says no!"

"Yeah, but Barry, 'no' could mean a lot of things to her," I explained being the marriage expert that I wasn't.

"Eh?" He looked puzzled.

"Well, when a bloke says 'no', it means no. That's it. No."

"Yeah..." A little understanding began to creep in.

"But maybe when she says 'no', it might mean she is embarrassed or somethin' and wants you to reassure her? You are her first squeeze after all."

"Ohhhhh!" not a fucking clue look on his face.

"Therefore, you have to gauge how she's feelin' talk about it more, be more sensitive, build up her confidence, ask gentle questions."

"Just fuckin' shove it in her mouth!" Russ added.

"Thanks Russ, fuck off!" I advised.

"Eh, why do men fart more than women? 'Cos they just day shut up long enough to build up the gas!" Russ delivered one of the few jokes that he knew and kills himself laughing.

"You don't fart much, do you Russ?" I added, leaving Russ looking confused.

"I just can't work 'em out, Dave." Barry continued.

"Who?" Sugar walked in with a handful of parts tickets sitting down at the workstation.

"Women!" Barry answered.

"You fuckin' white men, you are always tryin' to work 'em out!" Sugar spoke as he sorted the parts out and booked them in, "Save the effort, man, just say, 'yeah yeah yeah' to everything and let them get on with it."

"Oh, that's your philosophy, is it Sugar?" I questioned.

Chapter 17 - Sick and Relief

"Yeah, man. I mean, muff-divin'. What a fuckin' disgusting habit that is. Black men just don't do it, man. That's why some black women go after white men, cos they know you're gonna bite the beaver and no self respecting brother is gonna do it for em." He points a finger at us as he explains.

"Not your cup of tea, then?" I asked.

"No fuckin' way! Pussy is for fuckin'. That's it!" Sugar sucked his teeth.

"So, ya don't enjoy a blow-job, then?" Barry asked, intrigued.

"Of course I do!" Sugar didn't look up from his work.

"So what's the difference?" Barry tried to come over all politically correct.

"That's different." Sugar added.

"No it ay!" Russ shouts, "yem a male chauvinist ay ya!"

Sugar turned in his seat, getting up with his tickets in hand, "There aint nothing worse than a male chauvinist other than a fukin' woman who won't do as she's told!" With that he left the office.

"I suppose Ray's got a point. Don't even try!" I reflect. "I mean, when Tracy gets pissed off with me she says 'why don't you try and understand me' which means 'why don't you just agree with everything I say?'"

"Or, when she says 'there's nothin' wrong' it means everythin's wrong, ay it?" Barry was finally getting into the swing of it now.

"Yeah, like when I give her a cuddle and put my hand on her arse, if she's not in the mood she says 'why don't you just give me a cuddle without molesting me!?'. But if she's ten minutes off her monthly she will rip my kit off!"

"Yeah man, tell me about it!" Russ involved himself,

"The worst thing is when you've just emptied your sack and ye lie back ready to go to sleep and she starts fiddlin' about sayin' 'give us a cuddle'. I just say 'fuck off and gerus a flannel!"

"The other day..." Barry interrupted, "...she said 'can we do it again?'. I said, 'what do ya mean 'again'? I aye sixteen no more; yem getting' quality now, not quantity! She got really pissy about it!" Barry turned his eyes up.

"Then they say, 'are you asleep?' knowin' full well ye are! I'm sure it's not just me!"

"I blame them women-libbers" Sugar re-enters the office.

"Yeah, fuckin' lezzers the lot of 'em!" Russ agreed.

Now, I would at this point like to make it clear that I am in no way a chauvinist. I truly believe that women should have the same rights as men, but it just seems that some women only want to be equal when it suits *them*. Like those that are quite happy for men to buy them drinks all night, or pay for the meal, have doors opened for them etc because 'that's how you treat a lady'. Well, you can't have it both ways, can you? (Not meant in the physical sense!).

I am fortunate that Tracy is a true partner in every sense of the word. Even when we first met she insisted on paying her way. Having said that, even she enjoys the 'being treated like a lady' scenario which flies in the face of my understanding of equality. It's amazing how she uses the 'you're the man' get-out to avoid checking noises outside at night or getting the spider out of the bath.

When all the work was going on in our new abode, at one point we had pretty much every room being worked on by someone. During one of those particular days I was covered from head to foot in dust, paint and every other type of associated crap that comes from building work.

Chapter 17 - Sick and Relief

Tracy came home from doing something and I had the utter cheek to ask her if she could make everyone a cup of tea! Well! The teddies landed in most of the adjoining gardens as she argued:

"I'm not just here as the little woman to make tea, you know!"

"OKAY!" I snapped back, "Can you go and knock together that flat pack shed then? No? Well, how about moving that large pile of rubble into the skip? No? Don't fancy that? I know, how about pullin' down that "out house" then? Can't do that? Well, what would you like to do while I'm makin' the fuckin' tea, then?"

Silence.

It was at this point that an audience began to appear out of windows and around corners, as did my mother who took one look at the mess and said, "Come on Tracy, let's go and do some shopping". When the going gets tough...

It's fair to say that the male/female relationship was scrutinised on many occasions in similar forums. The scary thing was that by working in such a male dominated environment, I found my way of thinking being swayed to a more chauvinistic point of view. I'm glad to say that I have a healthier and more even view of the subject now I am a little older and wiser. I just say "yeah yeah yeah" and let them get on with it! [Thanks Sugar]

My fate had thus been decided and off I went a few days later to join Lloyd's merry crew, and had a whole new bunch of fuckin' maniacs to deal with.

Scattered around the New West were tall metal pillar-boxes with a computer terminal in each. All were connected to the main computer at the fifth aisle store. Drivers on the track ordered parts from the pillar-box terminals which would then be pulled at the fifth aisle by the store men. Before you ask, I don't know why it was called the fifth aisle, because there weren't another four!

The store area was a huge alley with over 500 pigeonholes measuring 3feet high and 6 feet wide. It reached a height of about 100 feet from the floor level which was 6 feet below the rest of the factory. It was a huge, cavernous place! In the pit itself, two drivers sat on 'sit and reach' trucks with the capability to reach the highest pigeonhole (be a bit stupid if they didn't!). At the far end of the alley was a small office for the drivers to have breaks in, which was great for disappearing into during the night as no one ever used it.

Working my shift was Phil, Fred, Harry and Paul. Paul was in his early twenties, quiet and unassuming, and he worked with Harry in the pit. Harry or 'H' as we called him was a mid-fifties monster of a man from Northern Ireland with a thick head of greying hair. In the holding area Phil and Harry commanded the movements and receipt of parts. Both were within a couple of years of retirement and neither gave a shit about management, and told them so on a regular basis whenever a manager would wander in looking for parts.

"If yam wants parts, order 'em like every other fucker! Now fuck off!" was Fred's favourite saying in his broadest Black Country accent.

"I'll report this to your line manager!" was the usual threat.

"The cunt is in his office over theya...give 'im my regards!"

Bearing in mind that you would probably have to back scuttle the Managing Director without permission to get the sack, threats like this were useless.

To add to his verbal ferocity, Fred was built like a rugby prop with a stomach like a beach ball. He was as

Chapter 17 - Sick and Relief

strong as an ox and would invite the younger workers around him to 'take the old cunt on' in just about any test of strength. Russ once decided to point out that Fred looked as if he had swallowed a wok and was duly invited to try and dent it. Now Russ fancied himself as a bit of a tough guy and did an 'Ali-shuffle' as he bounced towards Fred standing in the holding area.

"Are yem sure now? Yem an old fart and I day wanna hurt ya!"

"Come on, Skinny!" Fred encouraged, "Hit it as 'ard as yem can, but remember, if ye day put me down, yem getting' a forfeit."

"Yem won't be getting' up from this, ye old cunt!" at which Russ swung his right fist into Fred's substantial stomach with real ferocity, but with little effect.

"Okay, Skinny. Yem've had ya practice, now let's get on with it!" Fred pushed Russ back, leaving him with a look of concern on his face which turned once more to determination as he again punched Fred's stomach with his right, followed by a bonus left. Fred didn't budge; He just stood there smiling.

"Now for yem forfeit..." Fred walked towards Russ, "...I'm gonna turn ya into a time traveller!"

"Eh?" Russ looked confused.

"I'm gonna knock ya into next fuckin' week ye cunt!" Fred clarified. "Come 'ere ya skinny little twat!"

Fortunately for Russ, Fred couldn't run very fast so he managed to keep a good gap between them as Fred ran behind him laughing loudly. "Fuckin' kids!" he said when he came back, carrying on with his work.

Verbal exchanges of an abusive nature between Brummies and Black Country folk were far more frequent in this area due to the high volume of people from the said area working in such a small space. I'm sure that no love was lost between many of the opposing individuals, but on the whole it was accepted as the norm, and it never amounted to anything physical. It was generally a battle to see who could attain a higher intellectual plain, or in plain speaking, one would usually be trying to make the other look like a thick twat. I was drawn into many a verbal battle, defending my 'Brumminess' against the Black Country invader.

"I mean, you come to Brum for fuckin' work, so we can't be that bad!" was a usual knock back. (Pathetic really).

"It's only 'cos yem too thick te do it yemselves!" Would be Fred's rebuff, "And day forget it's all downhill from Quarry Bonk, so when I 'ave a dump it ends up in a Brummie resa (reservoir). Mind you, one of ma fudge brownies would be a square meal for some of you cunts!"

I usually gave up early, not wishing to be the centre of Fred's attention for the entire shift which could be a little daunting.

Needless to say, there was always going to be someone from either side that would show his compatriots up. There's been usually Russ, ours was, nine times out of ten 'Sharkey'. I don't know his real name, he was nicknamed 'Sharkey' because he looked like Burt Reynolds, or so I was told, when in fact he didn't at all! He was six feet, skinny, 25 years old with jet black hair. The only resemblance to his namesake was his thick caterpillar-like moustache, similar to those sported by Burt in the films, one being 'Sharkey's Machine' hence the name. To cap it all, he was very *very* thick which didn't help in his verbal exchanges.

Sharkey would lay into Fred or anyone from the Black Country at any given time, usually at break or the start of shift when his opponents would be gathered in numbers. I once witnessed him take the piss out of a

Chapter 17 - Sick and Relief

30-something driver called Gary who had recently moved his family to a bigger house in Wednesbury, just outside of Birmingham.

"Don't fuckin' start, Retard!" Gary threw the comment over his shoulder in Sharkey's direction.

"Woy? Are ya ashamed to admit ya live in that fuckin' shit'ole?" Sharkey responded, smirking at onlookers, seeking support.

"No," Gary replied, calmly, "It's because I've been to your house and I don't want to show ye up!"

"Fuck off, carpet fitter, yev only seen it from a minibus window in the dark!" Sharkey responded a little hurt.

Sharkey called Gary 'carpet-fitter' due to his large biceps and chest which prevented his arms from sitting flat against his body, leaving visible 'body-builder' gaps. Sharkey said it was because Gary's dad had forced him to carry rolls of carpet all day and his arms eventually stuck like that. Apparently, Gary's dad was a carpet fitter. Is this making any sense? Anyway, this was quite good for Sharkey.

"Yeah? and other than it being night, why was it so dark?" Gary paused, waiting for a response. "Because all the thievin' little Brummie fuckers had nicked the bulbs out of the street lights!"

"No...No..." Sharkey began to struggle, trying to think up a witty reply.

"Wrecked the suspension on the van pickin' 'im up! His road was like Baghdad International Airport after the yanks had finished!" Gary was rolling. "We drove past the local Dixon's [Electrical retailer] and in the window they had vacuum cleaners fitted with mud flaps 'cos the houses are so fuckin' dirty!"

Sharkey tried to laugh with the group to show he

wasn't bothered, but Gary went on...

"The local council started puttin' the gutterin' on the inside of the houses 'cos they were so fuckin' damp!"

Gary paused, looking at Sharkey and waiting for him to speak, but he just shifted from side to side as if trying to line himself up for a counter-attack that wouldn't come, but Gary was far too good.

"I hear the local council is tryin' to twin your town with La Treen in France ay it?" a loud outburst of laughter came from the group with Sharkey pretending to laugh the loudest.

"Yem day even know what La Treen is, do ye?" Gary asked, and Sharkey shook his head but carried on laughing. "So why am ya laffin'? Ya dopey fucker!" Gary asked.

"I don't know," Sharkey replied in a comical fashion which caused even louder laughter from the observers. Gary just smiled and shook his head at him with a hint of pity on his face. "Twat!" he said, and continued sipping his coffee.

Don't get the impression that Brummies and Black Country people were constantly at each other's throats, because they weren't. In fact I made many good friends from our Black Country contingent and had regular nights out there, sampling traditional ales which made me lose my ability to walk and speak after five or six pints. I also sampled many of the traditional Black Country dishes like faggots and peas, Kentucky Fried Chicken and McDonalds.

I made many acquaintances due to having to cover pretty much all of the jobs in the Fifth Aisle and driving jobs feeding the various parts of the track, and it was while I was driving that I noted the fact that parts from one particular supplier were always short. This was a real problem costing money during downtime when the

Chapter 17 - Sick and Relief

company was trying to operate the "just in time" system of parts ordering. This was highlighted to the relevant ears and I put in a suggestion to set up an area where the parts could be counted using a large set of scales that was left gathering cobwebs in the corner of the road receiving desk. Within a few weeks, an area near the Fifth Aisle store was put in place as were the scales, and each pallet was weighed to check if the correct amounts were being sent.

Now, a bone of contention for me was the fact that I had put this into the 'Bright Ideas' scheme, and when it actually came to fruition I heard rumours from those in the know that the supplier in question wrote a large cheque for previous misdemeanours. Thinking £5,000 reward, I awaited my confirmation from the top floor management which never came.

Eventually I approached the man in charge of the scheme who told me that my suggestion had already been under consideration so it didn't count! Needless to say, I pointed out how unhappy I was and suggested that the top floor were a little dishonest about the whole matter.

I was later given advice by my foreman Lloyd that the gaffers were a little unhappy about the language I used whilst explaining myself. Particularly the term 'Fuckin' robbin' shower of bastards' which I shouted in the corridor outside the manager's offices, was felt would not aid me in any future promotional aspirations. I do believe that Martin the Slimy shit head Hammersley [Remember him!] had some say in the matter too.

The counting jobs were in the main done by the people from the 'pool' which was the Old West training room. They were men and women close to retirement or between jobs who would wait to be used for short term things like this. Some people just enjoyed the regular change which kept them away from the monotony of doing the same task day in and day out.

I first met our counting crew when I was asked to take half a dozen pallets of material for them to check. As I pulled into the area, I noted a plastic table and four chairs had been deposited for the counters to sit on between jobs or during break times. The three of them stood, lined up, waiting for me.

"Where do ya want them lads?"

"Oh, just drop them anywhere," said one of the three who was wearing a white doctor's coat and holding a clipboard [Obviously in charge]. He spoke in a very well to do manner that surprised me as the shop floor was not the sort of place proper English was spoken very often.

His name was Phil and he was early-forties. He was a white male with a slim build and a balding crew cut hair style. He became known as 'Posh Phil' due to his accent.

Bill and Albert stood next to him and were a complete contrast. Both were in their sixties wearing blue company boiler suits. Albert was five feet tall, podgy with no neck or hair on his head. Bill looked six feet beside Albert, but was in fact of medium height. He wore a white cloth baseball cap which he never removed, and glasses that were so strong that if you looked through them with regular sight, you would be able to pick out intricate details of the moon's surface! So bad were his eyes that when he read a newspaper he held it within inches of his nose. Russ once commented on Bill's reading:

"If yem took them bottle bottom glasses off, yem might be able to read the fuckin' thing!" Which didn't go down very well as we all had a soft spot for Bill.

Following Phil's instruction, I placed the pallets on the floor next to the weighing machine, at which Bill piped up, "Ar, anywhere as long as it's not on my foot!"

Chapter 17 - Sick and Relief

and proceeded to burst into a fit of laughter which we all joined in with, not because Bill's comment was particularly funny, but because Bill had the stupidest fuckin' laugh I have ever heard! I will try to describe...

Imagine in your mind someone shouting "Yah! A" as loud as they can, and then repeating the 'A' about five times followed by a very loud 'O' pronounced as a small child would when learning the alphabet for the first time, then repeat about five times. Immediately followed by a 'Sid James' laugh, ending with a quietly spoken "Dear!" Add that laughter to a white cap and Japanese sniper goggles for the final image!

Albert followed Bill everywhere like his puppy. If you asked him a question he would smile at you without answering, or would make a soft giggling noise and mutter something. Bill usually translated for him. Posh Phil had to use hearing aids due to some ear disorder, and for work he had his 'everyday' set, rather than his 'best' set. He had one on each ear and I once asked him if they were designed by the people who made "spitfires" such was the antiquated style and size!

Fred and I wandered down to the store one day, sipping on a coffee, just to pass the time due to not much going on.

"Let's go and have a look at what 'hear no', 'see no' and 'speak no' are up to!" he said, which was particularly witty for a thick fuckin' Yam Yam. [I can say this now as Fred is on the other side of the planet and about 300 years old!]

As we got to the store I noticed that Posh Phil had a large spot on his nose that had been squeezed giving it a bright red glow that was very unattractive when teamed with his early morning baggy eyes. Fred must have noticed it too.

"Fuckin' 'ell Bill. I thought Dr Who 'ad killed 'im!" He shouted to Bill, indicating towards Posh Phil.

"Eh?" Bill looked confused, and Phil looked up from the pallet he was counting showing the large plastic aids on each side of his head, spotty nose and baggy eyes looking at Bill with a 'What's he say?' look on his face.

"Fuckin' DAVROS; Leader of the Daleks!"

Bill suddenly clicked and began to laugh, which in turn set us all off!

Having any visible characteristic was a sure way of being the subject of piss-take, but most gave as good as they got. Those that couldn't were on the whole left alone as we had unwritten rules even in this environment! Take Albert, for instance. The most inoffensive person you could meet, both physically and verbally. On his chin he had a huge black grape with three of the thickest black hairs you have ever seen, and I'm talking brush bristle thick, sticking out of it. I had this terrible habit of staring at it when we stood chatting, and the longer I looked, the bigger it got! Albert must have known people looked at it, but he never cut the hairs back, he just left them there.

A prime target for piss-take you would think, but he was left alone. [And before you say it, Austin 'fukin' Powers had not even been thought up at this time so I saw the 'Moley' thing first!]

Bill was also a very happy chappie with not a bad word to say about anyone. He was a lesson to us all. I found out that he had suffered a tragic loss in his life, which is his business, but which he shared with anyone who asked him about it. He was a practising Christian, but he never preached to anyone, and despite his appearance he was a very intelligent man proven by the fact that he was the only bloke in the place that did the 'Times' crossword. I had a lot of time for him and was chuffed when I heard

Chapter 17 - Sick and Relief

he had had a successful operation to improve his eyesight. Apparently he donated his old glasses to NASA to be used on a deep space telescope.

Another example of those that would be left in peace was a fellah known as 'Handbag.' No one called him by that name, and when in conversation he was always referred to by his given name. Fred introduced me to him one day, but not in the literal sense. I asked him why he called him 'Handbag' and it was explained to me in Fred's usual matter of fact way.

He told me that it was noted that Handbag carried a small bag with him at all times and one day it was dropped and a pile of tampax fell on the floor. According to the 'reliable' source it was explained that because Handbag was a 'fudge packer' and had 'been shagged up the shitter' so often, that his 'clacker didn't work anymore', the tampax was required to 'stop him from shittin' himself.' Brutal, however, he was an inoffensive soul and was left alone.

Like the pool workers, I was able to avoid boredom through a regular change of job that my sick and relief post provided me. I would watch the workers on the track and thank my lucky stars that I wasn't subject to such monotony. But for some, monotony or routine was the only thing that got them through the day! One old fellah I saw on the every day shift sat at his same machine welding a nut onto a 2 inch x 2 inch plate. That's *all* he did! And that's all I saw him do for four fuckin' years!

I once took away a small pallet full of the completed bits, replacing it with an empty pallet to be refilled. He mumbled something at me that I didn't hear and took no notice of as I drove off. A little later I saw him talking to a track foreman who looked up at me then came over saying "Can you make sure you put the pallet in the right spot for George, 'cos he gets a bit narked if ye don't!" or words to that effect. Now, bearing in mind that the pallet was no bigger than an apple box and weighed no more than 10kg empty, it was easily moveable by hand!

"You're havin' a fuckin' laugh, ain't ya?" I said incredulously, or would have if I'd known what incredulous meant at the time.

"You try getting someone else to do that fuckin' job, kidda!" was the curt reply, "just keep 'im happy for fuck's sake!"

I went back over and spent the next 5 minutes moving George's pallet back and forth asking him on numerous occasions "How bout here George, no? How bout here? No?" He finally threatened to shove his tea spoon in my anus, and I was bored any way, so I decided it was time to leave.

I found this with many of the people I serviced who had repetitive jobs. They liked everything positioned just so. This reduced effort and maintained a routine. One chap who worked on tailgate's told me that during an eight hour day doing the same thing over and over, grabbing 30 seconds to a minute here or there made all the difference to his sanity. I'm pretty sure if I'd ended up in a like job, my time and sanity at the plant would have been a lot shorter!

Now that I had changed my working area I was surrounded by people of a higher average age as opposed to the younger group on the deck. My new colleagues were in employment at the time of 'Red Robbo' and 'Leyland' and the attitudes that nearly destroyed the company were still present among them.

From a political standpoint I was usually at odds with almost everyone around me. I was 'blue' [even though I didn't know it at the time], where 90% were 'red'. This in

Chapter 17 - Sick and Relief

itself gave me a totally different attitude to the company than many around me. I would regularly pick up gloves issued to the workers which had been discarded around the floor or in pallets, in fact everywhere apart from the numerous glove bins provided for recycling them! By the end of the shift I would have a pile on my truck to dispose of properly, and it was on one of these occasions that a little tosser of a driver asked me in a sarcastic fashion, and in front of an audience, why I did this.

He was one of those blokes that you want to punch the shit out of on first sight. There was an attitude about him that made him think he was untouchable due to working in a safe environment where violence would result in the sack. He played on this, and often threw his unwanted penny into the conversation. Short and stout with a skinhead, as he was too tight to pay for a haircut, he looked way beyond his age of twentyish, and in some respects I actually think he tried to look older for some reason.

I pointed out the wider picture to him, of saving the company money by recycling rather than buying new, and that I was just trying to do my bit to help with the company profits. His attitude was 'fuck the company'. As long as he got his wages at the end of the week, he was happy. It was by this time that Fred and the Fifth Aisle crew had joined us.

I attempted to explain to the driver the cycle of buying, building and selling and all the things that add to the cost and which had an ultimate effect on profits.

"Yam can tell he's a fuckin' blue boy, can't ya!" Fred joined in, indicating towards me with his thumb.

"It's got nothin' to do with being 'blue', Fred, it's about makin' sure eleven thousand blokes don't end up out of fuckin' work 'cos of attitudes like dopey bollocks over there!"

The driver didn't react as he could see I was getting annoyed with the usual 'fuck the company' attitude.

"Yem all the same, fuckin' Tories; money first, people second me, me, me!" Fred walked off with Phil; laughing in the knowledge he was really winding me up.

I walked over to the coffee machine followed by Harry who broke the silence with his deep Irish accent. "Don't let him wind ye up, son."

"He won't," I replied, "I just get annoyed with the attitude of some people. I mean, half of these fuckers wouldn't know what to do if this place shut down!"

"They'll never close this place down!" Harry looked assured.

"H, we are a private company now, not Government owned! If we don't keep the Krauts happy they'll dump us like that!" (I clicked my fingers).

"No," Harry smiled, "The Government won't allow it! Too many people would be out of work!"

"I know you're wrong, H, but I really hope you're right!" I paused a second "I'm glad I won't be here forever. As soon as I'm back on my feet and got my head straight, I'm off!"

Harry looked at me with a knowing smile.

"It doesn't work like that, son. You'll be here ten years, then twenty. Before ye know it, that'll be it! Ye stuck here like the rest of us."

I don't know if it was the calm way in which he said it, or the fact it was getting close to autumn 1994 and the air was becoming colder, but I felt a horrible chill down my spine which I found hard to shake off.

"Not me!" I said defiantly. "I'm a mover, mate. I'm not gonna be here until I'm 65, and then die six months after retirement! I've got a life to lead!"

Chapter 17 - Sick and Relief

I threw my half cup of coffee in the bin and strode off.

CHAPTER 18

THE END'S IN SIGHT

"Keep roight on till the end of the road."
[A really annoying Birmingham City Fan]

Russ came charging towards me with foam coming from his mouth. He was as angry as fuck and looked like he wanted to hurt me. I braced myself but couldn't lift my fists up to lash out, I was frozen and defenceless!

"Yem a cunt; YEM A CUNT!" he kept chanting, his body turning into that of a pig and his teeth sprouting into large fangs through the foam.

I tried to run, but my legs wouldn't move. I felt the banister in my back, and as I looked I saw the abyss opening up behind me. Russ had become nearly all pig now and had blood all over his snout and fangs. He lunged at me causing me to lean back, putting my hands up to protect my face. The banister broke as he hit my chest and we began to fall.

"AAAAAAAARRGGGGGGGGGGHHHHHHH!!"

I crashed to the floor with a bump, my swivel chair lying beside me and the pile of plastic boxes I was using as a foot rest had scattered around the floor of the Old West receiving office. I rubbed my elbow which had taken the full weight of my fall, picked up my chair and sat back down, looking at my watch. 12:45a.m. and already I had fallen asleep.

I was working in the bowels of the Old West in a small office that had only one delivery per night, and that was it! I had already sorted the delivery, all but a few pallets remained to be stored away, but I left these just in case Lloyd came down so that I could tell him I was just finishing off.

So much sleep did I get covering this job that I didn't have to sleep during the day most of the time! No one was sick, and no one needed replacing which meant that I could disappear and no one would give a shit.

"I'm goin' to help them down the Old West." I would inform Lloyd.

"Yeah man." He would reply, waving without even looking, and off I would go. Fortunately, Mac and a few others were scattered around and Mickey Graham ran the show so he would pop in and buy me a coffee every now and then.

When I worked the 2pm-10pm shift I had the middle hours of the shift where I would be on my own in the Old West as the morning shift from there finished at 4.35pm and the night crew did not appear until 8.35pm. My job was to cover the gap. I would wander from work station to work station playing with cards left by the crews, or darts, and reading the day's discarded newspapers or flicking through the girlie mags left lying around. At the time I was into my second year as a military police reservist so I was into fitness in a big way, not to mention mental stimulation! I had the time to do both, using metal stairwells for pull ups and jogging around the outside of the building. I would spend hours reading quality newspapers [in between girlie mags] to improve my English, usually with the aid of a dictionary to help me through those ten syllable words.

It had been early May 1994 that I had applied to the local constabulary, my second attempt following one four years earlier. I didn't hold out much hope but thought it would be good practice for future attempts. Standards were high at that time and the Police was seen as a professional and respected organisation (the good old

Chapter 18 - The End's in Sight

days!). On reflection, I had it made. No stress or pressure, just turn up, fuck about, and go home. Mick even made sure I had the occasional Sunday morning overtime that was even easier to work than the normal hours!

I'd clock in at 6am, clear up the work that took me to about 06:30am. This done I drove up to the local swimming baths for an hour long swim, then back to the local café for a 'fat-boy' breakfast. I would return back to the office for a cup of coffee and a read of the paper so I was not late clocking out at 11am. Sometimes I even struggled to get it all in! Some may ask 'why would you want to leave a job like that?' Well, some are happy to have a simple life with no complications. But I needed, need, stimulation and I had to change my job for the sake of my sanity!

To my amazement I passed the initial Police exam, and as the months went on I got a little brighter and fitter which put me in good stead when the interview and the two-day assessments came around. On 23rd December 1994 I got my letter telling me I had been successful, giving me a start date of 23rd February 1995. It all happened so quickly, and was so unexpected.

I hadn't really prepared myself to succeed, so my decision to stay or leave had not really been thought through! Things were happening at work, I was taking German lessons due to the impending invasion (sorry!) takeover, with a move up the ladder in mind! I had also signed up to go on a six month operation with the Royal Military Police to Kosovo or somewhere the Red Caps needed filling out. I had a big decision to make.

One of the major driving forces I had for change was the untimely death of my mother-in-law Sue, who lost her battle against cancer on the 14th June 1994, a devastating blow to all of us. Even though we weren't exactly 'close',

I knew her for the best part of nine years and the grief that followed was utterly overwhelming. She was 49 years old, and it dawned on me how short life can be and that life is for living. (She is dearly missed).

As I pondered my decision over Christmas, I returned to work still unsure. Then I met up with Frankie Downs one morning in the small parts store. It was probably this coffee break that tipped me over the edge and made me realise that what I was doing was right for me then and for the future.

Frankie was 63 and a half years old at the time and had been at the plant since he was 16 years old. He was unmarried, lived alone and spent most of his time at work going from one little job to another that didn't take too much effort, but kept him busy. I believe that this job had been created for him due to his weak frame and age, so he had an easy ride into retirement. He had been offered voluntary redundancy at the time and rumours were rife about the huge sum he had been offered. All over the place blokes sat and tried to work out how many years he had been about and multiply that by the current yearly redundancy rate added to pensions and lump sums. The amounts for a working man were huge but little did they know what was going on in Franks mind.

We sat together as we sipped a hot drink and Frank puffed on one of his 20 foot long cigarettes he chain smoked. I could just about do one before turning green.

"Keep smokin' those Frankie and you will die an early death pal."

"Na son; I'm a bit loike that cunt Freddie Mercury when it comes te smoking."

"How so?" I said thoroughly confused.

"Well!" he settled as if about to offer the greatest punch line in the history of the Austin. "I know they are

Chapter 18 - The End's in Sight

gonna kill me in the end but I just love suckin' on me fags!" He laughed like a set of bellows.

"When ye off then, Frank?" I enquired shaking my head.

"Where?" He looked puzzled.

"V.R. Voluntary Redundancy. You must be worth a fuckin' fortune with the service you've got!" I clarified.

"Oh yeah." Frank told me the package he had been offered which would have set him up for the rest of his life quite comfortably. "But I ain't going'." He finished.

"What?"

"I ain't goin'!" he repeated.

"Ye fuckin' jokin' Frank? Tell me ye fuckin' jokin!" My plea must have looked very sad indeed.

"Nope. I'm stayin' here till I'm 65!" he said proudly.

"FRANK! FRANKIE!! FRANCIS!!! Are you out of your fuckin' twatin' mind?"

"Look, I'm happy here. All my friends are here" he explained "What 'ave I got other than the telly and me gardin when I leave ere?"

"Frank, you've only got 18 months left, and you'll lose thousands if ye just take ye pension!" I was pleading, "Think about what ye can do with ye redundancy money..."

"Nah!" he interrupted "Look at old Sid! He took 'is early and what 'appened to 'im? Massive 'eart attack within weeks 'cos of the shock to 'is system! I like my routine and I'm 'appy!"

I can't see the difference between a heart attack and a massive heart attack, I mean, they both kill ya! Tangent!

"But I doubt that was anythin' to do with retiring!"

It's a bit like 'chokin' on your own vomit. Who else's vomit are you going to choke on for fucks sake?

"Anyway," I continued, "He was gonna die at some

point, better spending his money than stuck in here, surely?"

"NO! Everyone's tryin' to get me to go but I'm stayin' till the death."

"Not literally, I hope" I joked.

"Ye daft cunt!" Frank smiled, swivelled in his chair and got up. He walked down the aisle with a box of screws followed by thick blue cigarette smoke. I watched him, thinking to myself *'Not me, man. Not me.'*

My decision was made, and midway through January 1995 I handed in my notice and the news that had been totally unexpected became common knowledge. I got the usual light hearted abuse as I had expected, but generally I was patted on the back for 'getting out'. There was a distinct reduction in the 'special offers' available to me around the place, but this was inevitable. Pete the hat was still happy to do business and even gave me a Police discount!

My last day came around and it was quite a sad time. I wandered around the New and Old West saying goodbye to faces I knew. Most of the time I had a lump in my throat and struggled from blubbering, but I knew that this would be the ultimate mistake. I was under no doubt that I wanted to go, but I felt very nostalgic about my time there and the people I met. If the truth be known I was genuinely fearful of what I had done. Here I was in a comfy world without a worry, and now I was voluntarily jumping into a world of rules and order.

After clocking off for the last time I was taken to the Austin Social Club by Neal, Alan, Geordie, Barry, Sugar, and a few others. They got me as pissed as a rat and left me in the safe hands of Macca! He took me to one of the roughest pubs in the area to continue with the drinking, telling all the local shitbags about my career change. How

Chapter 18 - The End's in Sight

I didn't end up naked and strapped to the bonnet of a stolen car I will never know. Due to my sentimental state I think I told everyone how much I loved them and would never forget them, this probably being my saving grace. How ironic that I locked a few of them up in the next few years. See! I never forgot them after all.

After a long stagger home, at some point I fell through the door with half a piece of fish and a few chips left in my paper for Anja, and I told her how much I loved her too.

After nearly five years, a mere drop in the ocean compared to some, My Rover Longbridge adventure had ended, and that was that! [Gulp]

CHAPTER 19

TO SUM UP

"Freedom!"

[Lots of people who've been locked up for a long time;
and Mel Gibson in an utterly fictitious movie about William Wallace.]

In today's society it seems very easy for people to say, you're only doing or saying that because I'm black, white, gay, pink or fucking whatever. This, in my lowly opinion, is a cop out much of the time and just serves to create bitterness. Many with dishonesty or personal gain in mind jump on the band wagon. Needless to say this tars those in minority groups who have genuine problems with the same brush, causing everything to get worse, not better!

I spent nearly five years working in close proximity with people from every culture, of every colour and background, in an environment that could be used by people from certain groups to declare institutional racism, or bigots stirring up feelings of bigotry. I never saw this, ever. I heard extreme opinions from many individuals and groups of course, but those opinions never seemed to isolate anyone or one particular group. Nearly always it was done in a non-confrontational light hearted way so that we could laugh together and lift the mundane atmosphere in which we worked.

Confrontation in a place with such a high volume of males is inevitably going to occur. However, I only ever had one physical exchange in all that time, with Sugar, and it is an amazing fact if you consider the potential for violence with a few thousand hot and tired males working closely together day in and day out.

Living in a Plant

One thing that always made my chest stick out was the unity we had if things needed to be changed. Everyone stood together even if the shit really hit the fan. This was in contrast to my following profession where those around you offer solidarity until it's put under pressure, then it's everyone for themselves. This, I'm sure, is not unlike most organisations where you have 'professionals' with a personal agenda, as opposed to shop floor, hourly paid employees who are happy to turn up take the pay and leave.

It doesn't matter how big or powerful the firm or organisation is; if the troops aren't happy and are united, then you had better listen, gaffer! Again, although it is a shame that this unity was abused in the seventies with the unions getting a bad name and losing so much public support. That same unity in any organisation today is seen as sinister, particularly in my new working arena. Management will do all they can to break up any non-work process related unity. As far as I'm concerned, this is a backwards step, because to promote unity in the right way will always produce a better work force, no matter what the organisation does.

I grew up a lot in those years and learned many new things about people and life in general. My appearance changed on many occasions as I went from a young man into a mature adult, although some would argue this point. My opinions on many things changed, most significantly my politics - going from a 'true blue' colour to more of a 'sky blue'.

I went from a 'Thatcherite' to a 'Blairite' [even though he hadn't been invented at that time]. I mean, what sort of bastard would take free school milk off kids and get rid of school dinners. Jamie, 'I'm gonna re-invent beans on toast' Oliver would have done his fruit and veg! [if he had

Chapter 19 - To Sum Up

been invented at the time]. Regardless of how I changed, I was accepted, not necessarily liked by everyone, but accepted none the less. Although I may have had a totally different outlook to many of those around me, it was never a problem.

My standard of living improved dramatically as money was good, with two house moves, a personally financed wedding and money in the bank for my change of career. (Oh yes, the Police salary was very poor!). I had personal time to modernise our very old home, visit the world a little and commit time to serve in the British Army. Most of all, I was afforded the privilege of starting a family.

I learned many new things watching and observing people, listening to different (sometimes extreme) points of view. This improved my interpersonal skills which aided me in my future life and career. It was another experience that made me the person I am today and I loved every minute of it. I hope you have enjoyed reading as much as I have enjoyed reliving it and writing about it.

It really was a different world in there and how easy it was to become a part of the community. I could imagine an alien visiting Earth and landing on the site. This little green man thinking it was the real planet Earth. It would certainly get an unusual picture of life, if it wasn't run over by a forklift truck when stepping out of the spaceship!

By the time it found someone and asked them to "Take me to your leader," it would be told in no uncertain terms: "Ye won't find any fuckin' gaffers now, son. It's after 5 o' clock, and anyway, it tay my job…"

'Q GATE'

CHAPTER 20

...AND FINALLY!

*"I would like to impress upon the people of this country
that if they have the interests of the nation at heart
and wish to see the solution to our unemployment problem,
the dole a thing of the past, prosperity a condition shared by all,
then they should see to it that it is a point of faith to purchase
nothing but the truly British article wherever and whenever possible."*

[Herbert Austin]

During 2005 the final death throes of the once great car company known as AUSTIN MORRIS, BRITISH LEYLAND, ROVER GROUP, and finally MG ROVER were heard and witnessed by the world. It was as sudden as it was shocking. There were no huge redundancy payments made as the money had all ran out, and thousands now found themselves kicked out onto the streets without a job.

John Towers and his consortium did everything to try and bring in foreign investment to save the day, and the Chinese were touted as the next saviours after the Germans and the Japanese had tried before. People cried out to Mr Blair PM to save the day with public money, but we all knew deep down that this would never happen. People marched on parliament and the papers drummed a beat in an attempt to keep the dream alive. The local historian 'Carl Fuckin' Chin' got on board telling everyone about the huge loss to our history it would be.

Surely it would be impossible to imagine that this great British Company would ever be allowed to disappear? All was in vain and in April 2005 the gates of

Living in a Plant

the last British owned Mass Production Car Company closed for the final time.

In 2007 the Chinese 'reopened' the Longbridge plant and started building MG sports cars. This was hailed as a new beginning, when in fact it is no more than a fraction of what Longbridge used to be. ROVER, the brand, is still out there and owned by someone, and you can still buy MG cars today. But, if you want a British mass produced car then you might start in the low end car sales pitches or the tat yards of the UK.

It was ironic timing that I left the UK for good in the hunt for a better life on sunnier shores with my family at the start of 2005, at the same time as the curtain was being drawn on the Longbridge plant. The difference in attitude towards home grown production in my new country to that of the UK was profoundly different. 'MADE IN AUSTRALIA' is a sign of pride seen in many places and on many products. Aussies look for it and buy it! What a shame the Brits could not follow this example, maybe then we would have a bit more 'MADE IN GREAT BRITAIN' left to be proud of.

I returned to the UK in the summer of 2008 for a family wedding, and on a day when I had little else to do I drove over to the Longbridge site to have a look and reminisce. It was about 2:30 pm when I arrived and the first thing I noticed was the complete lack of traffic.

Remember that this site ran 24 hours a day prior to closure and at this time of day normally it would be bumper to bumper with traffic, and full to over-flowing car parks. As it was, I was looking at a ghost town.

I decided to park up by Longbridge Rail Station and have a wander around, and see if I could get in or out of the plant. I entered the old North Works opposite the Station without obstruction and looked across acres of flat

Chapter 20 - ...And Finally!

concrete where buildings once stood. Parts of the building were still there but the metal pipes of different shapes and sizes that used to wrap themselves around the entire site, and protrude above the building line pumping foul smells into the air, were now gone.

I thought I could still smell the distinctive grey air that used to make your skin feel dirty just by walking past the buildings. However, the air was now a lot cleaner, and I thought that maybe this was just my mind telling me that's what I should be sensing. It was a hot day, and from memory these were the worst days for pollution in the past, but now the toxic steam that was once sent into the local sky had gone.

I walked along Longbridge lane towards the Old West and saw a banner covering the entire fascia of the building advertising a demolition company. Large signs said 'DO NOT ENTER' which I ignored. I walked in through the gates leading to the Old West Receiving Deck, opposite what used to be Longbridge Video Shop, but was now an empty shell.

Inside not a soul was to be seen, and how sad did I feel when I remembered how alive the place used to be. All those memories of events and faces were flooding back to me and I had to smile to myself as I sat on the benches outside the Old west receiving offices. All of it was destined to be torn down and forgotten. I contemplated walking up towards the New West but decided against it. I'd seen enough so I walked back to my car.

I drove along Lickey Road and up to Q Gate to have one last look then turned around and drove away, not expecting to ever again see the place as it was when I worked there. As I did I saw a familiar figure on a push bike wearing a 'post office' uniform carrying a bag of post. I stopped and waved at which the rider stopped

Living in a Plant

and recognized me. It was an old mate called 'Mark' [No not Madam Palms best customer] who I had spent many happy hours working with in the Old West and drinking with in the Old Rose and Crown in Rubery, just up the road from the plant. We shook hands and nattered about nothing much then went our separate ways. That was it for me, so off I went.

Word had it that IKEA were looking at building a superstore on the site where the North Works had been. How sad that 100 years of building cars could be replaced by a store full of women and gay men buying coat hangers called 'olaf' and chairs called 'ingerland'. There was also talk of a business park that would create more jobs than were ever lost by the plant. But would it have the same character? Not in a million years.

It surely makes no difference any more where your car is made, as the world is now global, and the Chinese and Indians manufacture pretty much everything we need. As long as it is cheap and economical most of us care very little. But where will the character come from? Does anybody actually care? I do, and even now search the local mags looking for an old Mini to do up just so I can drive it on a Sunday to the beach. I would suggest it certainly isn't just me, judging by the number of old cars still on the road that have been restored. Or is it just my age?

Perhaps the legacy of Herbert Austin will remain in our thoughts as the last of those vehicles built in his name disappear into the scrap yards, or decay under dusty sheets in someone's outhouse or shed. However, there is always a final twist in any good story. See, as the wreckers were tearing down the plant and its buildings, the 'shadow factory' of the war years began to reveal themselves and hold up the redevelopment.

In 1936 the British Government undertook a project

Chapter 20 - ...And Finally!

to build stuff for the impending war underground. This project was headed by Herbert himself, and one of the biggest was created at the Longbridge site. Tunnel after tunnel were revealed, much left as it was when the doors or lids were closed as Adolf ran to his own underground retreat. I would invite you to view online many of the incredible photos of this labyrinth that was, unknowingly, right under my feet.

Clearly the old site has a completely new dimension, and I am sure that those who value British heritage will see these tunnels as just as important as any war time historical place. Let us hope that the powers that be do justice to that history and allow the populous to see and experience this place.

I truly hope that in these pages you will be able to remember the old Longbridge Car Plant, and just as importantly the people who worked in it. I can say with genuine emotion that I really would love to be able to time travel and spend one more shift with those people. [Not the one where Sugar gave me a boxing lesson]. It really was something special and a genuine part of our heritage. In a 'modern world' where jobs don't seem to have any reason for being other than being a job [I have no idea what I'm talking about here but hope you do!] you cannot beat the image of people actually making stuff. In a culture of Political Correctness and being consistently offended at any cost, I hope you can chuckle in private at the absolute opposite that I experienced on a daily basis.

...and finally! If you ever manage to get your hands on a Rover Car made in Longbridge from 1990 to 1995, just remember that somewhere down the line, I put my hands on a part of it.

Cheers. Dave

Allegro, the square steering wheel. See, I wasn't kiddin'!

Bibliography

'Everyone who told me a story about the Rova' from 1990 to 1995.'

https://www.nation.co.ke/lifestyle/lifestyle/Meet-the-real-motoring-maestro-Herbert-Austin/1214-2507524-4ls72k/index.html

http://www.austinmemories.com/styled-10/index.html

https://en.wikipedia.org/wiki/Austin_Motor_Company

https://en.wikipedia.org/wiki/Herbert_Austin,_1st_Baron_Austin

https://en.wikipedia.org/wiki/Austin_Village

https://web.archive.org/web/20080910173708/http://www.lhi.org.uk/docs/Austin_village.pdf

http://www.austinmemories.com/styled-3/index.html

https://en.wikipedia.org/wiki/Longbridge_plant

https://web.archive.org/web/20120326141740/http://www.austinmemories.com/page113/page113.html

https://www.theguardian.com/politics/2017/nov/01/derek-robinson-obituary

www.ingramcontent.com/pod-product-compliance
Lightning Source LLC
Chambersburg PA
CBHW071908290426
44110CB00013B/1322